Happy is here

HENRIETTA SMITH

A life well lived

BY JUNE EHORN

June Ehorn

Henrietta Smith

CONTENTS

The girls at Fabiola gave Henrietta the name "Happy" many years ago. Our children benefited from her humor and ideas as she participated in some of their activities. She was our favorite neighbor and friend.

My husband and I were raised in San Francisco. We met before he was released from the Army Air Force during World War II, and we married in 1948.

Housing was hard to find as little had been built during the war years. Joe worked in Oakland and hoped we could find something there. Every day, he drove his mother to work and then across the Bay Bridge to his work.

Finding a suitable place to live was a constant source of stress and uncertainty. We found a studio apartment in Oakland and had our first baby, Scott, a year and a half later.

Not long after returning from the hospital with Scott, I received a visit from our building manager. He was apologetic but mentioned that most residents

June & Joe Ehorn

were elderly and that only a few worked. The baby's cry made it difficult for them to sleep.

We had dinner with Joe's aunt and uncle, who lived on 14th Avenue. Their young neighbor's house was for sale. It was a relatively new house with two bedrooms, one bathroom, a dining room, a living room, and a large, fenced backyard. However, it was located on a busy street with a bus route running through it. The price of the house was within our price range, $10,000.

We moved in on New Year's Day with the help of Joe's sisters' husbands. We didn't need furniture since Gertrude Otero, a cousin of Joe's father, and her husband Tom had furnished our apartment. They had raised Joe from infancy after the death of his mother.

We settled into the area. Joe's Aunt Lu and Uncle Jack were our neighbors. On the other side lived a blind couple. She was home every day while he operated a candy stand at the main post office in downtown Oakland. They were friendly, and we were amazed by their independence.

Two years later, our second son, Jeff, was born. The boys played in the backyard when they were two and four years old. Although they were safe, they did not interact with other children. Those days felt lonely because I had left my family and friends in San Francisco.

We were a one-car family, and I didn't drive. Once a week, I pushed the two boys in their stroller to the Dimond shopping district, bringing home groceries. Before shopping, we would walk up Dimond Avenue to the park at the end of the cul-de-sac. I did this while I was pregnant with Gail, and later with Lynn.

One day, while shopping, I read a notice in the library's window about a Cooperative Preschool. Even though the preschool was outside the area, I decided that if my children were to have friends to play with, I needed to take action regarding driving.

Joe worked from 2:00 P.M. to 11:00 P.M. each day. I asked Joe's Aunt Lou if she would watch the two boys while I took the bus downtown for driving lessons at a driving school. She agreed, even though she didn't drive either.

My driving teacher had an office on the same block as the Department of Motor Vehicles. He was an older man who used his car for teaching. I had to take my lessons later in the afternoon, and traffic was heavy. I sometimes had to drive along the train tracks leading to San Francisco. He had brakes on his side of the vehicle, although I don't recall him using them. After several days of instruction, he offered me his car for my driving test.

The first time I took the test, I passed! I was successful. I told Joe I had a driver's license the following day, but he was not happy. He told me we only had one car, so what good was it since he needed it to get to work?

I continued to follow up on my boys' preschool. They had openings and were happy to accept them. The school was located near Lake Merritt, west of our home, and towards downtown. We took the bus partway, and then walked several blocks to the school. Coincidentally, two other mothers were enrolling their boys at the same school. It was such a perfect day!

Joe's kind uncle gave us a well-used, second-hand car after hearing I had a driver's license. Now, I had transportation to the grocery store and could participate in the carpool to and from Tiny Tots. Our children attended there until they were old enough for kindergarten.

The preschool director was a family counselor and highly skilled in working with children. She held a monthly class for parents, from which I learned a great deal. The two women who also enrolled their children that day became my lifelong friends.

To actively engage fathers in the preschool, they were required to meet once a month on a Saturday to maintain the toys and equipment and to raise funds for replacements and the director's salary.

Fundraising activities included street fairs, See's Easter candy sales, wine tastings, and jazz concerts by Dave Brubeck, whose children also attended the school during our years there.

We spent seven years at this preschool, with all five of our children carrying fond memories and friendships that lasted into adulthood. It was wonderful!

Over time, especially after the arrival of our fourth child, our two-bedroom, one-bath home became crowded. In 1951, I had read in the news that the state planned to extend an existing freeway through our part of Oakland to connect with the entrances to the San Francisco-Oakland Bay Bridge. I had ample time to worry about that move.

2

In 1956, a representative from the Division of Highways visited us and informed us that our block of houses would be removed for the new 580 freeway, and that we would receive a fair price.

I knew where we should live: Dimond Avenue. I walked that street often, looking for "For Sale" signs.

I found two houses within a week. After telling Joe about them, we called the realtors. Both homes were on the side of the street bordering Sausel Creek, but we were looking for something different.

We entered the park to take the children for a walk. As we stopped outside the house closer to the park, an elderly lady asked if we were new to the area. We explained that the new freeway had forced us to find a new home.

She inquired whether we had seen the realtor's sign just inside the glass front door of the large house three doors down from hers.

We said no, and she gave us the realtor's phone number. We called the number she provided and arranged to meet him the following afternoon.

The house was built in 1908 by an architect from Scotland as a family residence. It had been vacant for two years. The builder's wife lived there until she was 96, having received assistance from a neighbor.

The lot measured 50 by 140 feet and included a two-car garage and 4,000 square feet in the two-story house.

The House on Dimond Avenue

It featured two living rooms, two dining rooms, two kitchens, and two spare rooms downstairs, off the driveway – one for storage and one for toys – plus five bedrooms, two and a half bathrooms, and two colossal date palms in the front yard surrounded by rose bushes. The living room windows curved outward, and the ceiling showcased large beams and a stone fireplace.

The living room featured dark-stained wood paneling, with a sliding glass pocket door separating the living and dining areas. A hallway entrance from the front door led to either the living room or the dining room. Both rooms possessed several intriguing characteristics. At the bottom of the stairs sat an old phone in a box that required winding to make a call. A bell in the center of the dining room floor was used to summon the cook. The living room showcased two glass sconces adorned with floral designs, concealing the gas pipes that passed through the wall to provide light.

In the backyard, fruit trees and blackberry bushes dominated the space. We acknowledged that most of the house needed attention before moving in.

According to the bank agent who assisted us, the price was set at $15,000 and was scheduled for auction. Joe appeared in court that day as the only interested party present. The bank raised the price to $16,000 to cover handling costs and the realtor's share.

I was incredibly excited, and my mother shared that feeling. In contrast, Joe looked worried and exhausted.

Our first task was to hire painters to refresh the living room paneling and beams. We chose a light tan color. My mother owned a business in San Francisco that produced custom drapes, curtains, and lampshades. She had her team create the draperies for the living room, ensuring they complemented the paneling.

Joe mentioned the house to his coworkers at the plant and the work he would do to make it livable. They began showing up on Saturday mornings for orders, refusing payment. They only requested hamburgers for lunch from the corner restaurant before heading home.

The dining room in the house on Dimond Avenue

The children, Scott, 8; Jeff, 6; Gail, 4; and Lynn, 18 months, were eager to see what was happening in their "new old house," a phrase coined by Jeff.

To keep them entertained, I took them to Dimond Park for

Saturday picnics, allowing them to explore what they could look forward to when we moved in: a swimming pool, tennis courts, swings, picnic tables, lawns, beautiful large trees, and a creek running through it.

There was an adobe building, the origin of which I did not know. I researched the history of the Dimond District and Sausal Creek to share with Scott and Jeff. I explained the park's vibrant history in simple terms.

Sausal Creek

Antonio Peralta inherited the property through a Spanish land grant from his father. It is now known as Dimond Park and the Dimond District and was subsequently owned by Henderson Lewelling. Hugh Dimond was born in Ireland in 1822. He arrived in America as a young man and made money in silver mining, the textile business, and the Gold Rush. When he reached Oakland, he had three children. In 1867, he purchased 12 acres of the Peralta grant, now known as Dimond Park.

The Adobe home was built in 1821. It burned down after many years, but the bricks were salvaged, and the structure was rebuilt. Adjacent to the building stood a massive oak, a sturdy, gnarled tree over 200 years old. In 1917, the city of Oakland acquired the 12 acres extending from Fruitvale Avenue to Lyman Avenue for $24,000 from the Dimond estate. The Oakland Park Department installed firepits for picnics. Sausal Creek was so clean that its water was safe to drink.

In 1924, Camp Sheoke was established, and the adobe building was transformed into the Boy Scout Headquarters. The director of Scouting offered a two-week campout for $14.00, which included meals in the 140-foot mess hall, access to the 300,000-gallon swimming pool, a bird sanctuary, and accommodations in 24 cabins and tents, along with an Indian Village where scouts could stay in tipis.

A military stockade was constructed at the canyon's summit, offering panoramic views of Dimond Canyon and East Oakland. However, plans for future canyon development were halted due to a funding shortage.

Adobe building

Hiking trails in Dimond Canyon remained open. Joaquin Miller arrived in the Dimond area of East Oakland, where he purchased 160 acres north of MacArthur Blvd. and planted trees in the heights. We enjoyed these trees while attending musical productions with our children on summer evenings.

In 1890, public transportation arrived in the area. At the foot of 13th Avenue, the first station was by the pier. The line terminated at the intersection of Fruitvale Avenue and MacArthur Blvd., where a turntable was situated. Horses pulled "balloon" cars, and passengers sat in a circle.

Along with transportation came a home for elderly German residents, situated on a hill overlooking the Dimond business center at 25th Avenue and MacArthur. I climbed this hill, pushing the stroller after shopping in the Dimond District while living on 14th Avenue.

Tepper's Hotel and Beer Garden was a fantastic resort where people from San Francisco vacationed in the countryside and enjoyed the outdoors, including a dance pavilion. This was a social hub for many years, and a short walk from what would soon be known as Dimond Park.

Our home on Dimond Avenue

It took six months to make the necessary changes to the house before we could move in. Neighbors dropped by and mentioned that they had considered the house, but felt it was too much work.

Joe's family (Gertie and Tom) had retired in San Francisco, and we offered them a unit in our home, which featured a freshly painted interior and a remodeled kitchen. In the backyard, they could garden if they wished. My mother provided drapes, curtains, and lamps for their living room.

June's daughters: Lynn and Gail

Tom grew zucchini until it became too large. We took pictures of the two girls holding them and settling into our "new old house," marking a new chapter for us as a family. For me, it was the most enjoyable life I've ever had.

3

———————

Seeing us in the front yard prompted our neighbor to come outside. She introduced herself as Mina Ols and mentioned that she lived alone with her cat. Opening cans was difficult for her, so Grandpa Tom offered to assist.

Her house had four rooms: two bedrooms, one bathroom, and a small kitchen. We often saw her walking down the street toward MacArthur Blvd., wearing a tall, faded blue hat and a long coat of a similar color. She always refused a ride. She would stop at the hamburger restaurant and the bakery next door for sweet rolls and cookies.

One day, she walked up the street and rang our doorbell, asking if Tom could climb in through her window because she had lost her key. We noticed her key hanging from a string down her back as she turned around.

A few days later, Tom asked me if I had seen Mina. I hadn't. We went over and rang the doorbell at the center of her door. There was no answer. I looked through the glass section of her front door and saw her on the floor, partly over her floor furnace. We went home and called the local police.

A single police officer arrived, a very heavy-set man. He asked for a ladder, so Tom went to our garage and brought one over. He was instructed to place it against the wall below a partially open window.

The officer asked me to climb the ladder, crawl through the window, and open the front door. When I reached Mina, she was conscious and asked me to find her address book on the kitchen table and locate Henrietta Smith's phone number. I was to call and inform her that Mina was being taken to Highland Hospital by ambulance.

The officer had called for the ambulance while I spoke to Henrietta in Fort Bragg. She was pleasant, but she explained that her husband was ill, so she couldn't leave at that time. I gave her the hospital's phone number and told Mina I had communicated with Henrietta.

Tom had barely put the ladder away when I saw Mina getting out of a taxi in a hospital gown. I was going over to lock her front door, so I followed her up the stairs. She seemed unfriendly and told me I could go home, insisting she was okay. I asked her if I could prepare something for her, and she loudly replied, "No!"

Later that day, while putting my laundry into the washer on the back porch, I noticed smoke coming from Mina's kitchen window. I hurried over, found the front door unlocked, and entered to discover Mina in bed and unresponsive. She had tomato soup burning in a pot. I called Highland Hospital again for an ambulance.

I contacted Henrietta to update her. She sounded tired and anxious, so I reiterated the situation to her. Henrietta shared that her husband was in serious condition.

I apologized for being unable to do more, explaining that I had four children and my husband's parents living with us in the house next to Mina's. I sensed her attitude shift. She said she would love to talk with me when she returns to Oakland.

This was my first conversation with an extraordinary woman who would have a positive influence on my life.

Henrietta called and let me know that her husband had passed. It was a couple of months before Henrietta moved into the house next door.

One morning, she came to my front door with her son,

Henry. He was over six feet tall, and she was a short lady about five feet tall. They both smiled and introduced themselves. I invited them in.

They'd had a long morning traveling from Fort Bragg. They welcomed a cup of coffee and mentioned that this was their first time in my house. Henry had flown from Woodland, where he lived, to Fort Bragg to pick up his mother. I offered a sandwich, but Henrietta said they had some business to care for before Henry left for home.

For several weeks, we saw little of Henrietta. She was in and out. It was nice to see the lights on again in the house next door.

Henrietta was alone most of the time. Whenever I saw her in her garden, I invited her for dinner. The family loved having her at the table. Her humor was infectious, and she had many amusing stories to share.

4

Henrietta's first story: Henrietta's parents, Emma and Luther, had been friends from childhood, having grown up on neighboring fruit orchard farms in Woodland, California.

Woodland is an area of trees and woods. German and other European people initially settled there. Due to the moderate climate, they could grow a variety of fruit trees. Henrietta's grandparents grew apricots and plums.

Emma and Luther married at eighteen years of age, told their families they did not wish to be fruit growers, and would live in San Francisco. Two months later, they left for new adventures.

Their new life started with a train ride from Sacramento to Oakland with $200 in Luther's pocket. They traveled to the dock to catch the ferry to San Francisco. This trip was exciting.

The evening fog covered the bay, and the ferry honked its horns. Approaching the pier, they looked up and saw the ferry building with its clock tower looming high above.

After arriving at the San Francisco Pier, hungry and tired from their travels, they looked for a place to get some food. It was getting dark, and they had no place to sleep.

A small café with lights on greeted them. A friendly waitress asked them to sit down as she handed them a menu. Prices were not high, so they ordered dinner.

On the wall was a bulletin board where strangers in town could post notes requesting reasonable living space, seeking employment, or seeking information about relatives who needed to contact them.

Luther noted a sign advertising a room for the night for $5.00, which included a bathroom and a coffee pot. The waitress knew and recommended the advertised room, as it was very close, just across the Embarcadero on the corner.

She said it would be best not to search for a place at this time of night. She asked if Luther was looking for work. He said yes. She noted that the railroad yards are three blocks away, and they offer fair housing options for families in the area. They thanked the waitress.

The next morning, they had breakfast after having a problematic sleep due to groups of loud drinkers outside. As they left the café, they walked to the train yards.

They found the office for employment and housing. Luther stated that they were 18, newly married, and wanted to live and work in San Francisco, and they had no family in the area. He was told they did not have an opening; however, they had temporary housing for a small fee. They were given directions to the housing area.

Emma and Luther walked west on Market to Third Street, then turned south onto Townsend. There, they noticed the warehouses, which consisted of several two-story buildings. The buildings appeared to be divided into flats, unpainted and poorly maintained. The streets in front were paved with cobblestones.

Emma felt disappointed as she looked at the area. There was a saloon on the corner where shouting and loud talking could be heard. The doors on some of the warehouses were open, and wagons were moving merchandise in and out of buildings.

A horse-drawn wagon carrying fresh vegetables and fruit was stopped in front of 506 Townsend, the address they were looking for.

A large woman wearing an apron and holding a basket was buying from the peddler. They approached her and asked about housing.

Emma was silent as Luther questioned the woman who introduced herself as "Mamy Brown." Her husband, Percy, worked at the railroad yard as a brakeman on the trains.

She then turned the questions to them. Did Luther have a job? Where were they from? Why had they left Woodland, and how long did they intend to stay? They expressed their wish to make San Francisco their home. They were recently married, and Luther was eager to work.

Mamy showed them an available apartment. It was on the ground floor. It had a small kitchen, a bedroom, and a sitting room about the size of the kitchen. A toilet and washbasin were in a closet off the kitchen. The apartment was sparsely furnished, but clean. The bedroom window looked out onto the street. Mamy quoted the rent.

She said that, since they had just arrived, they could pay their rent weekly for the first month. She had taken a liking to the couple, young and eager to start their life in the city.

Luther spoke as they returned to the café to retrieve their belongings. They had left two bags containing their clothing and wedding gifts, including a quilt made by Emma's mother and a leather-bound family bible from Luther's parents.

Luther noticed Emma's quiet, reserved attitude. He reassured her that this was temporary housing, and when he found work, he would find a house with a garden on a street without warehouses and saloons nearby. She smiled.

Henrietta continued the stories of her parents. She was born while they were living in the home the railroad provided. Henrietta said she had heard the story of her parents settling, or trying to settle, in San Francisco many times.

Luther left early the next day to purchase a newspaper and

check the job listings, many of which were far away. As the days passed, their little savings were slipping away.

Luther accepted day jobs. He often rose at 3:00 A.M. to appear at the wholesale farmers market to help unload produce from farmers or work as a stevedore unloading freighters.

Mamy became a kind, helpful friend, introducing Emma to the best low-cost food for her and Luther. She shared cooking utensils left by previous tenants.

Mamy loved having another woman to talk to. She had two sons, ages seven and ten. She walked them to school and met them after school. The closeness to the rail yards was a concern, as the boys were always curious about the engines and the "treasures" carried in the boxcars.

Emma had been taught to sew by her mother. She had made her two house dresses and her one best dress. Her mother had taken her shopping in Woodland to the mercantile store the month before her marriage to purchase material. The patterns were cut from newsprint.

It was extraordinary to have bought fabric. All her life, her clothing had been made from feed sacks, a common practice when you lived on the farm. The scraps were used for quilts.

On Sundays, if Luther did not have work, they would wear their best clothing and walk up Market Street, looking in the shop windows. The Emporium, the largest store on the street, sold beautiful clothing.

The summers in San Francisco were cold, unlike those in Yolo County, where farmers and orchard owners welcomed the hot, dry heat. The fog sometimes covered San Francisco for days. Mamy gave Emma a small, worn, wool shawl to keep her warm on those cool days, and she was happy to have it.

As jobs were scarce for Luther, he wondered if they had made a mistake leaving the farm. Their letters to their families were filled with the sights and sounds of the city and the pleasant people who owned their homes. They said not a word about their work or their worries.

Emma felt she needed to help with their living expenses. She cared for Mamy and Percy's two boys when they went out on a Saturday night, but she refused payment from them because of their kindness and friendship.

On one late-night walk, she saw a sign in a window advertising a job at the Emporium. The next day, she put on her best dress and walked into the women's wear department. A sign read, "Help Wanted in Alterations" in the Better Dress Department. The woman who stepped forward to meet Emma wore a plain black dress. Her blonde hair was pulled severely back into a chignon. She spoke with a French accent. Emma felt like a country girl as she sat down to talk with the department manager.

She looked directly at Emma and asked about her experience with the job. She explained that their customers in that department were some of the city's most influential and wealthy women. Some of their customers were stage, theatre, and opera performers. She explained that they were entrusted with beading, fine silks, and lace gowns.

Looking at Emma, she said, "What experience do you have that I can entrust you with these costly gowns?"

Emma spoke quietly and said, "My mother taught me. I made the dress I am wearing."

Seeing no response, she stated, "I need a job. My husband has had trouble finding steady work."

Emma was asked if she had children. She responded, saying, "No, but we plan to start a family one day."

The woman stood and offered her hand to Emma. "I will give you a chance to show your ability. Report tomorrow morning."

Emma returned home, elated by her success and her

newfound ability to help Luther and ease some of his stress. He arrived home near dark, his clothing dirty. He had found a job digging trenches for a new sewer system about two miles up Market. He was to report back in the morning.

Emma told him about her day. He did not appear overjoyed.

"My wife is not supposed to work outside our home," he said.

Emma said, "I want to give it a try! They may not keep me there, but I must try my best."

The next day, Emma put on her best dress and walked again to the Emporium. Her first day went well as she replaced hems and moved buttons on more beautiful gowns than she had ever seen. At the end of the day, Suzanne, the department manager, told her that the job was hers. Emma was delighted.

As the months rolled by, finding jobs seemed more challenging for Luther. Emma's salary soon became the primary source of their support.

One November morning, as Emma arose for work, she felt uneasy in her stomach. She left for work without breakfast and made her way to the store. It was raining. A loaned raincoat from Mamy kept her partially dry on the long walk.

When she arrived at the store, Suzanne stopped and asked her what was wrong. Emma rushed to the restroom to vomit. She washed her face and suddenly felt faint.

Suzanne found her on the floor, noting her wet stockings, shoes, and the same dress she had worn on the first day of work. She offered her a cup of tea and told her she was taking her to her apartment a block away on Mission Street and giving her a change of clothing.

When Emma returned home that day, Luther was sitting at the kitchen table. He was unable to find work and did not want to discuss it.

He asked Emma how she could afford new clothing, noticing the more stylish dress she was wearing. She told him of her day.

As they spoke, there was a knock on their door. It was Mamy holding a pot of stew for their dinner. Percy was home for a day, so she had made extra food for his next run on the freight train heading for the San Joaquin Valley.

Emma thanked her but told her she had been feeling ill since the morning. Mamy smiled and asked her if she could be with child. Emma could not answer. While she and Luther discussed having a family, this was not the right time.

After Mamy left, Emma served each of them a bowl of stew. They sat in silence during their meal.

As they cleared the dishes, Luther said, "If we have a child, we will have to return to the farm, tell our parents we have failed to make our way here, and live with one of our families for a while."

Emma flushed and said, "We will not go home and say we have failed. We are going to succeed here in San Francisco!"

Emma was reluctant to tell Suzanne she was pregnant, fearing she would lose the job she so desperately needed. Mamy had altered dresses she could no longer wear for Emma, given Emma's widening girth.

It was as though she had a new sister. She showed Emma how to put together the basic needs for her expectant baby. She contacted the midwife who had delivered her two sons to be aware of a pending call.

Luther's frustration with finding non-permanent jobs was apparent as he frequented the saloon across the street. Emma discussed her concern with Percy. He told her he would inquire at the union office to get Luther a job.

It was March of 1896. Emma had trouble getting up from the floor after marking hems on customers' dresses. Suzanne asked Emma why she had not discussed her pregnancy, and Emma shared her fear of losing her job.

Suzanne reassured her that she did not wish to lose her. Emma continued to walk to the store. It took longer, as she often had to stop to rest.

Luther was offered a job as a signalman on the freight train that Percy worked on. They made runs to Southern California, sometimes being gone for several days.

5

―――――――

It was a windy and cool June day. Emma had missed the last two days at the store because she did not feel up to walking there and back.

She called Mamy to ask about the midwife. "I think I need help," she said. Mamy took off her apron and, with her youngest son, hurried to 5th and Howard to Mary O'Leary, the midwife. Mary grabbed her satchel and went with Mamy.

Emma had partially undressed and was lying on the bed as the pain was becoming more severe. She suddenly felt a warm rush of water, and her bed was wet. Emma was frightened, saying, "Why didn't I let my mother know that I was expecting a child? Why isn't Luther here?" Mamy arrived with help. She and the midwife comforted and coached Emma.

After nearly 12 hours, a baby girl was delivered. Her eyes were so black, and she had little hair. "She will probably be as blonde as her parents," Mamy noted. The baby was bathed and wrapped in a recovery blanket Emma had made. She was so beautiful. Emma smiled at Mamy and said, "Wait 'til her Daddy sees her!"

The summer passed. Emma returned to work after three weeks, and Luther continued working on the railroad. They decided to visit Woodland to see their families and introduce their daughter, Henrietta, to her grandparents.

It had been a year. The family seemed glad to see them, but still could not understand why Emma and Luther had chosen to live in San Francisco rather than in the country and Woodland.

Mamy took care of Henrietta when Luther was on a trip. Luther loved his baby daughter, but again grew restless as Emma saved her money and spent it carefully.

She received a tip from an appreciative customer. She put that money aside, saying, "This is going towards a home of our own." She asked Luther to look for an evening job when he was not on a train trip, but he refused.

Luther started frequenting the saloon across the street. He said he had friends there who also worked on the freight trains. Emma told him this practice upset her and was not strengthening their marriage.

He teased her about the wealthy people she worked for and said maybe she thought she was better than the people who were their friends on Townsend Street, an area known as a "shanty town" by those who lived near the hills and Van Ness Avenue.

These conversations became hurtful, so Emma avoided discussing Luther's drinking.

In December of 1897, Luther was fired from his train job. He had shown up for work drunk. They told him they could not take a chance with a drunken man.

Christmas arrived. The store had been so busy. Emma worked long hours altering high-fashion gowns for the wealthy's holiday parties.

Before she left the store, Suzanne handed her two gifts: a French doll for Henrietta, now 18 months old, and a gold flat box containing a lace handkerchief embroidered with bold lettering for Emma. It was indeed the loveliest she had ever owned.

Emma walked home among the Christmas shoppers, anxious to see what Luther and Henrietta had done that day.

She stopped at a chocolate shop and bought a box of chocolates for Mamy, Percy, and the boys.

As she entered the flat, it was dark. She called, but no one answered. The music from the saloon poured into the quiet, dark street. Emma removed her coat and took the box of candy to Mamy.

As the door opened, Henrietta yelled, "Mama, Mama," and toddled to Emma. Mamy told Emma that Luther had asked her to watch Henrietta so he could buy her a gift. He had not returned. Emma thanked her and wished her family a happy holiday.

Emma had purchased a watch with a chain for Luther as a Christmas gift. She had made monthly payments and thought every railroad man needed a watch. The chain clips through the vest buttonhole and hangs down; the watch is in the vest pocket. She envisioned him taking the watch out and checking the time.

Back home, Emma warmed some soup for Henrietta and herself. She felt lonely, remembering the preparations and happy times growing up in Woodland.

She bathed Henrietta in the kitchen sink and dressed her for bed. Emma sat with Henrietta in her arms, singing a lullaby. Henrietta was soon asleep.

Emma prepared herself for bed and worried about Luther. Maybe he had an accident. This would have been a lovely evening of shared gifts, and knowing they did not have to get up early and report for work on Christmas Day. She dozed off as she lay in bed. She had left the lights on.

After midnight, she heard someone trying to put a key in their front door. As she opened the door, the smell of alcohol was strong. Luther was leaning against the door jam.

Emma had trouble controlling her anger. The late hour kept her from raising her voice. Luther stumbled into a chair.

He said, "I went shopping for a gift for you, but all the stores were closed." Emma closed the door and told him they would talk in the morning.

Christmas Day was quiet for Emma and Luther. After breakfast, Luther shared the gifts from their families in Woodland. Henrietta loved the boxes and wrapping and amused herself.

Emma handed Luther the gift she had purchased for him. As he opened it, tears welled in his eyes. "But I don't have a gift for you." He admitted that he no longer had a job with the railroad.

Emma sat on the floor at his knee and said, "You can give me a gift, a promise of sobriety, and an earnest effort to find steady work." He leaned forward, kissed her, and said he would try.

Emma was busy at the store during the week between Christmas and New Year's Day. Holiday parties required new dresses.

Luther kept his promise but had no luck finding a job. They quietly celebrated the new year, promising a better year and continuing to value their life together.

6

For ten years, there were reports of unrest in Cuba. The newspapers reported on a pending war as the new year began. Accounts were circulated involving Spanish cruelty to the citizens of Cuba. Some called the stories the result of "Yellow Journalism."

Still, following the explosion of the US Battleship "Maine" in Havana Harbor in 1898, President William McKinley believed the American people favored intervention and declared war on the Spanish army in Cuba.

A ship loaded with food and supplies was sent to Cuba for the Cuban and American soldiers. They were forced to sail around the island for a week.

On June 27, 1898, after the Rough Riders had taken the first strategic spot of the war, Clara Barton and three Red Cross nurses set sail in a small boat. The hospitals were under the control of a Cuban general. They found soldiers on dirty floors, with only army rations to eat.

On July 1st, they were overflowing with angry casualties from the Battle of San Juan Hill. Food intended for them had not arrived. Conditions were terrible; patients were without clothing or food and suffered from malaria.

Luther walked into the Emporium the day after the war was declared to tell Emma he had enlisted. He would report to the Presidio for training in the morning.

Emma was speechless. She had been altering a gown for a

new customer, Emily Harris, a singer in a club on the Barbary Coast.

Emma told Luther to go home, take Henrietta home from Mamy, and stay with her until she could get home to help him prepare to leave them. Emma apologized to her customer and explained her absence. Emily liked Emma and told her she understood.

Emma's life changed after Luther left for training. He visited from time to time as the training center would occasionally close.

On the last Saturday in March, Luther arrived at the store at closing time and told Emma this was his last leave before boarding a troop train heading for Florida and the War Front in Cuba.

Emma and Luther spent their Sunday with Henrietta, traveling to Golden Gate Park. Emma had packed a small lunch and a shawl. They boarded the streetcar, which took them west towards the ocean.

Henrietta chased the birds and loved the feel of the grass under her feet. Emma and Luther laughed as she ran, turning to see if they were watching.

Luther became serious and said to Emma, "If I do not return, I want you to promise me you will return to Woodland to our families. I could not bear the thought of you raising Henrietta alone here in San Francisco."

She told him she would think about it. He had told her he wished her to go to Woodland on his enlistment. Emma became angry at that suggestion, telling him he had signed up without discussing it with her. She would not leave her job or her friends at this time.

Little mail came from the battlefront. Emma read the daily newspaper to stay informed about the war's progress. She read about a U.S. blockade of Havana that went into effect on April 22, 1898.

She also read about the ship that left the East Coast filled with supplies and food for Cuba to assist the starving reconcentrados women and their children who were put in prison by the Spanish.

The food and supplies were distributed to the Cuban and American soldiers. The reconcentrados were 400 miles away. Clara Barton, a famous nurse, traveled to Cuba in 1898 to help the Cuban people.

Luther's letters were short and included little news. He was not accustomed to the hot and humid weather. He had been involved in minor skirmishes, but reassured Emma he was not injured. He missed her and Henrietta and asked her to write more, as he had received letters from her that were three or four weeks old.

On June 24, 1898, the Rough Riders had taken the first strategic spot of the war. Luther was chosen to join this group. After the battle, Clara Barton and three Red Cross nurses were encouraged to stay on the ship but went ashore in a small boat.

The hospital was under the control of a Cuban General. On July 1, the hospital was overflowing with ongoing casualties from the battle of San Juan Hill.

Luther wrote to Emma, describing his experiences on the battlefield. His right leg was shattered, and he had Malaria. He told her of Clara Barton's help to the wounded. "She is an Angel of Mercy," he wrote.

Emma wept as she read his letter. "How long before he is home? Will he come home?" she asked herself.

Emma felt the love and support of Mamy and Percy. Suzanne offered dresses Emma could wear to the store and surprised her with clothing for Henrietta. The families in Woodland always encouraged her to come home.

In November, Luther was sent home. He had spent months in Florida in poor conditions while waiting to return home. He was told he was not well enough to travel. Dysentery and malaria took many of the people who had survived the battlefield, but many did not survive the pitiful conditions in Florida.

Emma was there as the train pulled into the Townsend Street station. Ambulances lined up from the Presidio hospital to take the injured and sick there for further treatment. People crowded around the station.

Seeing Luther's condition was a shock. He was thin, his skin was yellow, and a blanket covered his legs. As Emma looked closer, she realized he had only one leg.

Five days passed before Emma was allowed to visit Luther in the hospital at the Presidio. She was ushered into a crowded ward. Beds lined the walls.

He cried when he saw Emma. "Where is Henrietta?" he asked. "Why didn't you bring her so I could see her?"

Emma told him she felt she was too little, and since he had been away for so many months, it was best to wait until he could come home.

Emma asked him about his leg and why he had not shared that information. He told her how ill he had been with malaria, which may have been from mosquito bites. Emma was still confused. They had experienced mosquito bites growing up in Woodland, but it did not make them ill.

Emma visited with Luther, reassuring him that all was well with her and Henrietta. His family in Woodland would come to San Francisco to see him when his mother was well enough to travel. She explained to Luther that his mother had been very ill while he was away.

As she walked down the hall, Emma stopped a nurse and asked for the name of the doctor who was treating Luther. She directed her to an office with a sign on the door: Major Herman

Olson, M.D. She knocked and was asked to enter. A fatigued, short, balding man introduced himself to Emma and asked what he could do for her.

Emma told him her husband's name and said she was there for information on his condition and how long before she could bring him home. Dr. Olson went to his files and removed Luther's chart. He asked Emma to have a seat and allow him a moment to review Luther's records. He stated that his caseload was heavy.

When he turned to look at her, she knew from his expression that what he would tell her was not good news.

He started with, "You know your husband had his left leg amputated in Cuba under poor conditions following his injury. It has not healed as it should have. There are several reasons for that. His poor nutrition on the battlefield left his body compromised. By that, I mean he was not able to ward off what happened to him as he lay in the hospitals in Cuba and Florida; he contracted Bacillary Dysentery, a dangerous, highly contagious bacterial infection."

Dr. Olson went on to say, "This is often the result of poor sanitation. Flies may have spread it, contaminating food and water and resulting in symptoms such as fever, nausea, and vomiting, which can weaken patients. Luther was also infected with malaria. He received that from a mosquito bite. This enters the bloodstream and travels to the liver. Some patients recover from this; its symptoms include high fever, chills, and uncontrollable shaking. Others may have a more severe case, causing liver failure and death."

The doctor paused, seeing Emma pale and shaken. He rose and called the nurse to bring Mrs. Smith a drink of water.

He continued, "When your husband is released from here, he may need constant care. If you have children at home, I will consider other care for him."

She explained that she has a young daughter and works, but does not have enough money to care for both Luther and Henrietta.

Dr. Olson assured her he could stay at the hospital until he could help himself move from the bed to the chair. He said he did not think Luther would make a complete recovery. She should be prepared for that eventuality.

Emma did not remember her trip home from the hospital. Her life was changing. She greeted Henrietta with a hug and encouraged her to play while speaking to Mamy. Mamy offered her a cup of tea. They talked, and Mamy assured her that Percy and she would be there to help them as much as they could.

Emma went to her flat and broke down in tears. A feeling of hopelessness swept over her. She lay down on her bed and curled her body, her arms around her legs. When she awakened, it was dark.

The weeks passed. Emma made her way to the Presidio on Sundays. When the weather permitted, she packed a picnic and prepared a small lunch, taking Henrietta to see Luther.

The nurse wheeled his chair out onto the wide porch facing the bay. They spent some happy hours together. Luther seemed to tire quickly. Henrietta constantly talked and laughed to be the center of attention. Luther called her his "Shining Penny."

Luther was released from the hospital the week before Christmas. His mother had passed away in Woodland before she was able to see her son. Luther's father arrived to spend Christmas with them. He stayed through the holidays but was anxious to return to the farm. He had carried gifts from Emma's family and an invitation to return to Woodland, where they could assist in Luther's care.

Mamy watched Henrietta, now nearly three, and brought lunch to Luther, stopping to see if he needed anything.

During the day, Emma was so busy working long hours at

the store this time of year. The customers were pleased with her alteration work. Suzanne encouraged her, and Emma gave orders to temporary seamstresses hired for the holiday rush.

The strain of work and caring for Luther, both before and after work, began to take its toll. The bright spot in Emma's day was watching Henrietta share her play with Luther and seeing him smile. He watched as Emma bathed and prepared Henrietta for bed. Emma would hum and hold her until she was ready for sleep.

Luther had episodes of returning malaria symptoms. On these days, Emma stayed home to care for him. Luther would become so depressed as he saw Emma doing her best to care for their little family and support them financially.

He would say, "I should have died on the battlefield." Emma would cradle his head and try not to let him see her tears. She saved those for the darkness when she couldn't sleep and wondered what would happen if Luther were taken from them.

As the weeks passed, Luther's body became so weak that moving from bed to chair had become impossible for him to accomplish alone. Emma would fix his breakfast and take Henrietta to Mamy before leaving for work.

Mamy reassured her that she would check in periodically, and Percy would sit with him when he returned from work.

One cold February evening, as Emma entered the flat after work, it felt so cold. It was dark, as no lights had been turned on. Luther was in bed and appeared asleep. As Emma approached the bed, she realized he was not breathing.

Luther had lost his battle for life. Luther's father returned to San Francisco to bury his son at the Presidio Cemetery. Percy and her father-in-law handled the details.

7

The years since Luther's death had been difficult for Emma. She had developed a following of customers, and in exchanges of pleasantries, they would ask her about her personal life. Did she have children or a husband? She was reluctant to share this information with strangers.

One customer she met in her early days at the Emporium was Emily Harris, a singer at a club on the Barbary Coast. She was outgoing and kind and had brought flowers to Emma following Luther's death.

After learning of Emma's and Henrietta's birthdays, she never forgot them. She would come to the store with a gift in her hands. She often told Emma about other housing options that might be safer and more pleasant for her and her daughter.

Emma would thank her for her consideration, but she could not leave Mamy and her family. They had become like family, and she loved them.

Emily often invited Emma to the club to see a new show she was part of, but Emma declined. She mentioned these invitations to Mamy, who told her she should consider an evening out, as Luther would want her to enjoy her life.

Emma agreed to accept Emily's invitation if she and Mamy could go as well. Henrietta could spend the evening with Mamy's sons, who were now old enough to watch her for the evening.

Accepting Emily's invitation, they took the streetcar and

walked a few blocks to the Lucca, a club in the middle of the Barbary Coast.

As they entered the club, a large man with a big smile and hearty laugh greeted them. Emma told him they were Emily's friends and had come for the show.

He grabbed her hand and introduced himself as Mac, the club's greeter, bartender, and a friend of Emily's. He winked at them and said, "Someday, she will be my wife."

Emily and Mac

They thoroughly enjoyed themselves and were pleased to hear Emily's beautiful voice.

Mac's laughter, as he mingled with the crowd, resonated in the club. She thought, "What a cheerful man. They would make a wonderful couple."

8

Henrietta was nine and doing well in school. Her ready laugh and friendly manners made it easy for her to make friends. Mamy's two sons treated her like a little sister. Sometimes they teased her, but they were always protective of her.

Henrietta had stopped asking about her father. Emma had taken a photo of Luther in his uniform before he left for the war. She put it in a large frame and hung it on the wall. It was visible as soon as you entered their home.

When business was slow at the store during the summer months, Emma took Henrietta on a ferry and train trip to Woodland to spend a few weeks on her grandparents' farms.

The family looked forward to their visit but missed them when they left. They always encouraged, but never insisted, that Emma and Henrietta return to Woodland to live. Emma's parents were in poor health.

Luther's father had passed away in June the previous year. The farm was given to his brother. In recent years, the brother had three sons working on the Brown farm and Emma's parents' neighboring farm and orchards.

Her parents had told her in their last letters how much they appreciated their help and wished to make compensation to them upon their deaths. They assured her a sum of money would be paid to her and hoped this arrangement would meet with her approval.

San Francisco had changed since Luther and Emma's arrival in 1895. It was an actual city. The opera house and city hall

39

were imposing buildings. Many men had made their fortune in railroads and silver mining, while others watched their fortunes grow on the Stock Exchange and in real estate. The natural beauty of its location made it a sought-after destination.

The morning of April 18, 1906, was a date that would never be forgotten. Emily and Mac had announced their engagement and invited Emma, Mamy, and Percy to join them for a special dinner and celebration at the club on the evening of April 17, 1906.

Emily gave Emma a dress she had worn once, hoping Emma would wear it. Emma looked lovely in the soft blue folds of silk, a beaded bodice, and a sheer shawl of silk draped over her shoulders.

Emma's blonde hair was always braided and rolled. This night, her hair was rolled and held in place with a pearl-and-silver-encrusted comb, a gift from Suzanne. Emma felt beautiful and wished she were sharing this evening with Luther.

Suzanne had asked if Henrietta could spend the night at her apartment. She would share her doll collection with her, and Emma could come for Henrietta the next morning. Emma agreed.

The buildings shook. People were familiar with earthquakes, but this was different; they took immediate action. With difficulty, Emma made her way to Suzanne's apartment to be with Henrietta.

She had just reached the Townsend Street entrance when another great movement occurred. Screaming and yelling, people rushed out of buildings. They were in the 1906 earthquake.

It was dangerous to walk the streets as parts of tall, ornate buildings fell and windows shattered.

Arriving home with Henrietta, Emma realized her home had been destroyed.

Fires were seen in the distance. The military set backfires to slow the progress. The army was actively involved in setting up tents in Golden Gate Park and throughout the city, providing meals for those in need and facilities to maintain cleanliness and promote good health.

Many hurried to leave the city by ferry boat. The army realized they could not let men capable of working leave the city. Women and children could leave if they had a place to go. Men were only allowed to leave with a pass issued by the officer in charge.

The next morning, the officer in charge called for attention. Trying to ease people's anxiety, he ordered all men, young or able, to do a day's work searching for residents stranded in damaged buildings or homes.

He told the women with children and those without families to come forward and receive a ferry pass for the boats to the East Bay.

The first boat going to Oakland took women and children, landing at the 13th Avenue Pier. Employment opportunities were provided, along with childcare for their children. The day consisted of working in a cotton mill founded by sea captain John Yule Millar in 1883. William Rutherford joined him, and textile manufacturers organized investors.

The most crucial enterprise was in Oakland, employing 150 people. The mill helped cotton farming in the state. Their early products included grain sacks, sailcloth for salmon fishing in the Pacific Northwest, towels, and damask, which was distributed in the U.S. The building had 3,800 windows.

Emma thought it best to stay where she could receive shelter and food for herself and Henrietta. After several days, Emma received a pass for her and Henrietta to go to Oakland.

The ferry tied up at Pier 13, and Emma joined the line of women with children in their arms or at their side.

9

———

Upon arriving in Oakland, Emma was enrolled and placed in an area to work according to her sewing abilities. She was then directed to the payroll line to sign up for payment at the end of the week.

A friendly older woman identified herself as Mina, the head bookkeeper. She asked a few questions about their experience in San Francisco and whether more of her family would follow. She told her about her husband's death and that it was just her and Henrietta.

"Do you have a place to sleep here?" she asked.

"No," answered Emma. The woman smiled at Emma and said, "I have a spare bedroom you may use until you settle. We will contact the local school for Henrietta. I will meet you outside at the end of the day. It is quite a walk, but it is still light outside."

Emma thanked her for her generosity toward her and Henrietta. With their workday over, they walked together and chatted about their lives. Mina had never married. Her father had taught her bookkeeping so she could get a job and support herself.

Emma and Henrietta stayed with Mina until Emma was able to afford a tiny house on Fruitvale Avenue within walking distance of Henrietta's school.

On Saturday nights, Emma and Henrietta walked to Mina's house for dinner on Dimond Road.

After dinner, they would sit on the front stairs and listen to

43

the music coming from Tepper's Open Ballroom, see the camp-fires in the open space, and smell the cooking from the camp-fires near Sausal Creek. Families were enjoying their time outdoors, some coming from San Francisco.

They always enjoyed these Saturday nights at Mina's, but the happy atmosphere seemed different this week.

After dinner, Emma suggested that Henrietta go out and listen to the music while watching the campers arrive to set up their tents.

She heard Mina and Emma talking in low tones. It was the beginning of many times when she was left out of their conversations.

Emma asked for shorter hours at the cotton mill. The person who gave her instructions on her work asked if she was well. Emma told her she had cancer and should probably quit her job.

Emma finally told Henrietta that she was seriously ill. They would have to make some changes to their living arrangements. Henrietta was silent, but said she could take care of her mother.

Emma told Henrietta, "School is the most important thing for you, and Mina will bring you to visit me on weekends when I'm in the hospital. We will live with Mina for a while. You have two more years until you enter high school. During the summer, you will visit your cousins in Woodland. You will make new friends and make plans for your future life."

Emma only lasted two months. With her mother's passing, Henrietta felt a profound loss. She continued to live with Mina.

10

Henrietta started high school and found it enjoyable. She made friends and found science classes that interested her in her quest to follow her dream of becoming a nurse and helping patients recover.

She made a special friend, Ruth, who shared her interest in nursing. Mina approved of her inviting Ruth to stay some weekends and Henrietta visiting Ruth at her home on other weekends.

Life was a simple challenge for the girls. Going to nursing school was the plan.

Following high school graduation, they applied to Fabiola Nursing School, the only hospital and nursing school in Oakland. They felt fortunate to be accepted.

Fabiola Nursing School

The Fabiola Nursing School was opened in 1876 by 18 women. Each gave $50.00 to secure a five-room house. It was called The Oakland Homeopathic Hospital and Dispensary.

Fabiola Hospital

In 1883, it outgrew the space, and a new hospital was built. The hospital was renamed Fabiola Hospital after a noble Roman matron from the 4th century who opened her home to the poor and the sick.

Henrietta and Ruth read in the newspaper about Mother Jones and her efforts to find justice for those wrongfully imprisoned. She had done great work in Mexico to find solutions to the imprisonment of Mexican Patriots.

They discussed her efforts, and Henrietta and Ruth hoped to follow her example someday.

Mother Jones

Mother Jones was one of the most picturesque figures in the American Labor movement. She was a crusader. She was interested in ending child labor in the eastern coal mines. Attention was drawn to the six-year-olds employed in cotton mills to pull threads and replace spindles on 8-hour shifts at ten cents a day.

She often fought without success. Boys were hired to work in the coal mines. They worked in areas where coal chips and dust were present.

After eight years of work, the Western Federation of Miners Union successfully improved working conditions in Idaho, reducing the workday to eight hours for adults and eliminating child labor.

Miners built stores, opened libraries and hospitals, and established funds for widows and orphans. Much of this was accomplished through the efforts and publications of Mother Jones.

Henrietta met a doctor at the nursing hospital. All the girls talked about dating him. When he asked to take Henrietta for a row on Lake Merritt, he got fresh, and she tipped the boat over. A newspaper said, "A doctor saved a nurse from drowning." But, actually, she had saved him!

Henrietta read about the plans for the 1915 Fair and Exposition to be held in San Francisco. It was to be called the Panama Exposition, celebrating the completion of the Panama Canal.

Henrietta and Ruth were saving their money to attend the fair, take the ferry boat to the Palace of Fine Arts, and see the beautiful plants surrounding it.

As she read from time to time about the planned large buildings, the plans for the Palace of Fine Arts, designed by Bernard Maybeck, held her attention. It would house thousands of paintings. A tower called the Tower of Jewels would have cut glass of various colors to catch the sun during the day and the light at night. It was said the tower had 102,000 pieces of Bohemian glass.

Buildings showcasing culture, music, and the fine arts would be surrounded by spacious, beautiful gardens. Sculptors and painters with worldwide reputations were hired to participate. *(See Appendix A for more information about the Exposition.)*

Henrietta and Ruth acquired programs for the upcoming fair as soon as they became available. They were amazed by the variety of attractions. They planned a list, realizing there was more than they could see in a day. Admission was fifty cents.

Henrietta and Ruth planned their visit for their first weekend off, deciding to stay until closing and enjoy the sights. The fair was crowded, so they had to save some sights for the next time.

The trip back to Oakland was a new experience. The fog had come in, so the ferryboats went back and forth with their horns blowing and all lights on. They decided their next trip would be in the daytime.

Their time in school was becoming more complex and requiring more study. Time was becoming more precious. A few girls were leaving to get married or pursue different occupations.

Henrietta always tried to get a Saturday off to spend time with Mina, filling her in on the latest medical information she had learned. She also stayed in touch with family in Woodland.

After two years of learning and hiking in the Oakland hills with the girls, the classmates felt close and joyful.

Papa Doc was a highly respected doctor at the nursing school and a kind, caring man who never hesitated to listen to or guide each nurse in deciding her future.

Completing their required course of study, Henrietta and Ruth would read and study Mother Jones's work and discuss it with "Papa Doc."

After the graduation ceremony, he congratulated the girls and asked them if they were still interested in Mother Jones. They told him they were.

Papa Doc and nurses

He said he was traveling to Mexico to investigate the conditions of American citizens being held in prison. Some had been wounded in battles against the current leader, Diaz, who was known for his cruelty toward both the Mexican peons and the Texans who had come to Mexico to oppose his regime. *(See Appendix B for more information about the Mexican Revolution.)*

They felt honored to be asked to accompany Papa Doc, and they were given instructions on what to wear. He packed all the medical supplies they would need for the prison. The girls had no inkling of what they would find. Some prisoners were near death due to a lack of water, food, and improper treatment of wounds.

Henrietta and Ruth were relieved when the doctor announced they could go home after a week of work. He felt they had done all they could considering the conditions they found.

Papa Doc thanked them for their help and wished them good luck in their chosen field. He told them he would report to the U.S. Department of Health in Washington, D.C., so they would know the conditions they found in the prisons.

11

———

After their final trip to the fair and the completion of their training at Fabiola, Henrietta and Ruth met to discuss where they would look for jobs.

Henrietta had read in nursing publications about hospitals that were short-staffed. She was interested in a job offer in New York. This hospital provided training for midwives and offered surgical care to patients. She showed it to Ruth, who told her she did not wish to go so far away from her family.

Henrietta told her she understood her feelings. "I only have Mina and some cousins I am not close to in Woodland." Henrietta sent a letter to a hospital in New York City.

Henrietta received a letter from the hospital recruiting office, informing her that they were hiring. They wished to meet her, review her grades at Fabiola, and get two recommendations from her instructors. Henrietta took her letter to Mina to read and ask for her opinion on the offer.

Mina told her that it must be her decision. She felt confident that she could succeed in all her new ventures.

"I am proud of you," Mina said.

Mina told her she would finance her trip to New York, but that was all. Then Mina said, "When you inquire about the job, ask for help with your first month's wages and housing."

Henrietta secured her recommendations to be sent along with the grades for her two years at nursing school. Within two weeks, she had her acceptance.

They offered her the cost of travel and housing for the first month. She went to see Mina and thanked her for her support and care since her mother's passing.

She called Ruth and asked her to meet her for lunch. They talked and laughed about their high school years and the Fabiola days.

Ruth had found a job at a hospital in San Francisco. She could live at home. They hugged each other and promised to stay in touch with letters as much as possible.

The train ride from Oakland to New York was long, but Henrietta walked between meals each day and found several women traveling alone who were talkative and friendly; however, no one was on a mission similar to Henrietta's.

12

———

On arrival, Henrietta took a taxi to the hospital, where she was assigned to provide nursing care to patients hospitalized for various reasons.

After three weeks, Henrietta went into the head nurse's office and asked when she would be assigned to midwifery. The nurse behind the desk told her that, based on her experiences on the nursing floors, she would be asked to advance to midwifery. She realized that Henrietta had another week before that was possible.

On her off time, Henrietta read in the hospital's medical library. Learning about the history of midwifery was a helpful experience. Native Americans had midwives. It was noted that Bridget Lee Fuller had attended three births on the Mayflower and was recorded in The Diary of Martha Ballard about midwifery in 1785-1812 in the Colonies.

After each day's reading, the subject matter made Henrietta more anxious to be put to work in her chosen nursing field. She was interested in reading about the scientific side of infectious diseases. This information was not included in midwifery but was covered in obstetrics.

Henrietta was told that her work as a nurse in the hospital was well-received, and she could move into the midwifery section. She was informed that the hospital's doctors do not accept midwives. The wealthy who could afford a doctor did not want a midwife.

Henrietta was sent to the floor to care for the patients who had delivered their babies by their favorite doctor. She never mentioned midwifery to them.

Although she was beginning to realize that the midwife was not accepted by doctors in large hospitals, midwifery services were needed by people experiencing poverty.

The hospital sent her to a clinic in the poorest part of New York, known as the Bowery, to be trained as a midwife.

Often, the living quarters were not clean, and they housed large families with many children. The children looked poorly, and the mothers were ill. The fathers were unskilled. Too many used their low wages to buy alcohol instead of food for their families, were wounded on the job, or were not able to pay for care.

Her calls as a midwife were few and far between. When she was through delivering, she would return to the hospital.

13

There was some joy in Henrietta's work as she was invited to some of the nurses' homes. These families looked well and loved having Henrietta tell them stories about California.

One of the families had a son in a hospital in England. He told them about a friend who had been a flyer in the Royal Air Force but was shot down and did not know when he could go home. This family said their son would be coming home when transportation was available.

Henrietta returned to her routine of hospital care and occasional visits as a midwife in the poorer areas of New York.

One morning, she noticed a sign on the coatroom wall. It was from England, requesting nursing assistance from nurses in the United States. World War I was still going on. They had a large group of American wounded and not enough nurses.

Henrietta thought of her father and his time at the Letterman Hospital in San Francisco. She noted the return address on the sign.

During her lunch hour, she wrote to the office. She informed her head nurse that she had applied for a nursing position in England, and the head nurse asked if Henrietta had thought her move through.

Henrietta said, for personal reasons, that she felt she was making the right decision.

Henrietta received her acceptance letter from the military office responsible for recruiting medical personnel.

She had a week to prepare herself for her embarkation. She

would be traveling by transport ship, and only one piece of luggage was allowed.

She was to appear at the medical office for a physical exam. The boat was leaving at a time not to be disclosed to friends or family.

14

Henrietta did as she was told, though she had some apprehension; it was a new experience on a ship with the lights out at night. Military supplies took up most of the space.

She began to think of what she would do when she arrived in England: write to Mina, Ruth, and the family of relatives in Woodland, visit the son of her nursing friend who was hospitalized in the military hospital, and write his family a letter to ease their worry about him and his English friend.

After settling into her sleeping area on the ship and learning the meaning of the bells at different times, she was comfortable, except for the ship's rocking after they were out to sea. Fortunately, nausea was not a problem for her, unlike many passengers.

After days at sea, everyone was glad to hear the English port was in view.

She traveled in a small bus, along with some of the other passengers from the ship, to a large building on the edge of town.

Two soldiers were on the porch to provide information to those entering. With their help, Henrietta found a nursing employment office. She was told they were glad she had answered their need for additional help.

Uniforms and work schedules were issued. She would be placed with the American injured as much as possible.

Since language would not be an issue for her, she was told that she would occasionally care for British service members.

She assured them that she was happy caring for all those in need. She mentioned the name of a nurse's son in the United States who was hospitalized there.

"I was asked to see him and send his mother a note telling her of his progress and possible date of discharge."

The next morning, Henrietta was called back to the office. She was told that the patient she asked about was doing well, and he would be happy to have a visitor from home. His discharge was still not known.

She handed Henrietta a paper with his name and room number. Before starting her day, she found the room and introduced herself. It was a two-bedroom.

Not knowing him, she called out his name.

He answered with a smile. "In my mother's last letter, she said I would have a visitor. See, I told you, Henry, I was going to have a visitor from the U.S."

In the next bed was a young blond man who appeared very tall. He smiled and waved his arm.

It was near check-in time for Henrietta's workday to start. She returned to the office and told the nurse she had met the young man and would write to his mother.

"I am ready for work." She was given a list of room numbers and patients, more than she had ever received for a one-day job in the U.S.

At the end of her day, she always went by the American soldier's room, smiled, and talked to the two young men for a while. They were so pleased with her visit.

The U.S. soldier had received his orders to return home. His roommate seemed sorry that he would lose his friend. They exchanged addresses so they could stay in touch.

Henrietta told the English patient she would continue visiting him at the end of her workday. He was pleased to hear that. Her smile and cheerful attitude brightened his day.

15

The first day after his roommate left, Henry looked forward to that smiling, friendly nurse who would make her way to his room at the end of her workday.

He asked her to pull up a chair and sit closer so they could talk and get to know each other. His dinner tray arrived, and he wanted to share it with her. She told him he needed his strength and the nourishing meals sent to him, but if he would like, she would bring her dinner tray to his room, and they could talk and enjoy their meal together.

He said that would bring joy to his day.

They had dinner together that first evening. He asked Henrietta about her life in California. She told him about her parents growing up in Northern California, on acres of fruit trees in Woodland.

After her parents married, they traveled to San Francisco. Seeing the lit clock tower on the San Francisco Ferry Building brought them joy. It was modeled on the Bell Tower of the Cathedral of Seville. Ferries plowed the fog-shrouded Bay, traveling from East to West.

They settled in San Francisco, where her father worked on the railroad. Her mother found work altering women's clothing.

Henrietta continued, "I was born in their small living quarters. My father joined the army during the Spanish-American War. He was seriously wounded and passed away when I was three years old. I had a close neighbor caring for me while my mother was at work. The 1906 earthquake destroyed our home. We lived in Golden Gate Park with help from the Army and the Red Cross. We were given passes to board a ferry to Oakland across the bay. Work was available for my mother at a large cotton mill. Childcare was offered. A kind woman, the bookkeeper of the mill, offered us her spare bedroom until we settled."

Henrietta told him she wanted to hear about his life.

"I am sure it is more exciting than mine." He said he enjoyed hearing about her.

Her life was exciting to hear about. His nurse entered the room and informed him that his visitor had to leave. He was due for dressing changes and a back massage.

They sadly said goodnight. "I will see you tomorrow. We will continue our story."

The following afternoon, Henrietta made her way to Henry's room, her tray in hand.

"Hello, I am ready to hear your story," she said with a smile.

Henry's tray was before him, but he had not touched it. She smiled and said, "How has your day been?"

He responded, "I've been waiting to see you, and hoped you hadn't forgotten our plan to have dinner together."

She said she would not have done that to him. She pulled her chair close to the bed, moved the food on his tray to make it more convenient for him, adjusted hers, and said she was anxious to hear about his life before he became a pilot and entered the war.

He began his story with his childhood, growing up on a sheep farm and helping his father with daily chores. As he grew up, his father gave him more responsibility. He took him to meetings with other sheep owners.

"In our area, we grew the Ortum Flock of Pedigree Suffolk Sheep. They had long bodies and long white hair. Their wool was considered the best by knitters and manufacturers of high-priced knitwear. We lived near open fields with varied vegetation to encourage the development of large, healthy sheep. We lived a few miles from Lincolnshire, an area with a long and fascinating history."

William the Conqueror founded Lincoln Castle in 1068. He could not have dreamed that today Lincolnshire would be a place of historic houses representing every past century. Visitors can now find clean beaches, rolling countryside, unusual gardens, stunning houses, traditional town markets, and an antique hunters' paradise.

Henrietta was so impressed by what she had heard that she told Henry she wanted to go to Lincolnshire when he was released and able to walk.

Henry explained that the Suffolk sheep growers refined their techniques.

"I loved the whole process. There are inspectors to make sure they receive the best care."

Henrietta said, "I have learned a lot, but I would like to know how you became a flyer in the Royal Air Force."

He smiled and said, "That is a long story. When I was about sixteen, I became interested in flying as planes flew over our farm from a faraway airfield. Cranwell College was nearby, and it became a Royal Air Force (R.A.F.) training center."

Henry was nearing the age of acceptance for the service. At the airfield and college where flying was taught, he watched the activity in the air and wanted to be part of it.

A few of the hired workers with the sheep were leaving to join the armed services. With the sheep's birthing season, they had a problem feeding the young animals.

It was decided to contact the high school to arrange for volunteer students to bottle-feed the young lambs.

<h1 style="text-align:center">16</h1>

When Henry reached the acceptable age, he enlisted in the Air Force. He was allowed to join the R.A.F. for training.

After months of schooling and flight training, he knew he loved the process and felt ready to do his part for his country.

After flying missions for several months, he was shot down by a German pilot. He told himself, "If I recover, I will fly again."

Henrietta smiled and told him she was proud of his achievements. "You are fortunate that your injuries, from what I know, will heal with time by doing the required treatment your doctor orders. I will see you tomorrow at the same time. Rest well!"

Henrietta kept her promised visits and told him about her days with Fabiola. Five months later, Henry was told he could be discharged if he had help at home and transportation back to the doctor's office for checkups.

When Henrietta made her daily visit, Henry gave her the news, and she was pleased. She leaned over and kissed his cheek. He grabbed her arm and told her he could not imagine his life without her. He did not mean as a nurse, but as a wife.

He told her he had grown to love her. She smiled and told him she felt the same.

Henry said he would call his parents and ask about a wedding at their family church if that was all right with her.

She would make her request to leave the hospital, and live at the farm until the war was over, and he could travel to California. She would help him follow the doctor's orders.

Henry's mother answered his letter and said that arrangements would be made at the church on a day to be decided. She and his father were anxious to meet the American nurse he had fallen in love with.

We want you and Henrietta to feel at home here until it is safe for you to travel. Henry's parents spoke to friends in the area and at the church about Henry's upcoming marriage to the American nurse who had cared for him in the hospital.

Henry was given an approximate discharge date. After receiving that information, Henrietta put in her request to leave the hospital. All went well.

17

The ambulance delivered Henry and Henrietta to the farm. His parents were thrilled about the changes that would take place in their home. They greeted Henrietta with happy smiles and outstretched arms.

Henry's mother took Henrietta in and showed her their guest room, which, for now, was meant for her. She was shown a cheerful room with a large bed and a beautiful quilt, lovingly made. She could see the extensive green hills and valleys with the white sheep grazing. This welcome brought tears to Henrietta's eyes.

"I wish my mother could see this," she said to Henry's mother as she fought back tears.

Henry's father took him out on the farm to see the changes. The wheelchair was brought to help Henry get back to the house.

The wedding was arranged. Friends of Henry and family were invited. Some had seen Henry grow up. Henrietta told his parents to hold off on a wedding date until he felt stronger.

It was May before the wedding took place. A reception was planned under the blossoming trees. The guests were friendly and kind to Henrietta.

She had written to Mina and Ruth, as well as her cousins in Woodland. She also contacted the family of Henry's friend from the hospital to give them the news.

Henry continued to recover and spent much of each day with his father. When he was able to walk, his dad drove the four of them to see the historical part of Lincolnshire and had lunch at a restaurant in town that the family had loved to patronize when Henry was growing up. The restaurant owners were happy to see Henry. He introduced his American wife. His parents told them Henrietta was a nurse in the hospital where Henry was recovering from his war injuries.

This was the beginning of the kindness and friendship Henrietta enjoyed as time passed with his family.

With the end of the war and the return of steamship travel, Henrietta discussed a trip and possibly moving back to the U.S. with Henry.

He told her he would investigate the move. "We should not call it permanent until we can support ourselves." She agreed.

They told the family they were considering taking a trip to the U.S. and seeing the lady who had raised and supported Henrietta in all her choices, her only friend who attended school with her and went to nursing school, and her family in Woodland, who had taken over the orchards after the death of her grandparents.

She mentioned this trip to Henry not because she was unhappy in England, but because of those people she had left there, and she missed being home in California.

Henrietta knew this would be difficult for Henry's parents, as he had only been home for a short time. She promised they would return soon if they could not support themselves in California.

Henry's parents were quiet after their talk, but said they understood Henrietta's wish to return.

"You know you are both welcome any time. We consider you a daughter already, Henrietta."

It was late July when they made their reservations to go to the U.S. One evening, as they were packing, Henry's mother came in with a beautiful shawl on her arm. She handed it to Henrietta and sat on the side of the bed.

The shawl featured a paisley design in a tear shape. The scroll pattern is adorned with a leafy motif that dates to the 11th century in India.

In the 15th century, elite European women sought the Kashmiri paisley shawl. Queen Victoria bought 17 paisley shawls in jewel tones in the same century. Before long, Victorian women wore or displayed them as art, draping them over chairs, tables, or pianos.

The Kashmiri paisley shawl

This shawl that Henrietta received from her mother-in-law was a treasured gift. They packed the shawl carefully. Henrietta put her arms around Henry's mother and told her that she would treasure it always.

They left early to drive to the pier where the ship was being prepared for the long trip to America. When it was ready to leave, the horns blew. They stood on the ship waving to Henry's parents on the shore and shouting, "We love you!"

The trip was smoother than her first.

Henry said, "It's too bad. If we could fly, we would get there sooner."

Henrietta thought he was teasing her, but his love of flying was always present as the years passed. They arrived in San Francisco and took a ferry boat to Oakland.

Upon landing and getting their luggage, they looked for a telephone booth and called Mina. When she answered the phone, she was so pleased to hear Henrietta's voice. She told them they could have one of the bedrooms if they wished to stay with her until they decided where they would settle. They accepted.

The few days with Mina were cheerful. Mina filled Henry in on her time with Henrietta when she was a young girl.

Henrietta called her cousin in Woodland. She informed him that she was married and that they were considering living at the orchard.

She reminded him that it had been left to her by her grandparents. She had left the farm because she had felt that she could not take care of the land by herself. "We are not trying to move you off, so we would like to sit down and discuss things with you."

Henrietta told Henry that she felt her cousin sounded cautious while speaking to her.

Henry said, "It is understandable since you have been away so long and now you've come back saying you want to take over."

She wrinkled her face and grabbed Henry's arm. "You are right about Woodland."

They took a bus to Woodland and walked out of town to

the farm. The flower gardens were no longer around the house. Growth was wild around the fruit trees.

They went to the front door and knocked. A man came to the door. Bearded and untidy, her cousin, Sam, apologized for his appearance. He invited them in. They could see a woman in a wheelchair, who did not look well.

He introduced his wife, Sara, to Henrietta, and in turn, she introduced her husband, Henry. They sat down, and Sam talked about why everything looked neglected. He said they had experienced a dry year.

The cost of water had gone up. He had needed to let his two helpers in the orchard go. Sara has been ill for the past two years.

"I understand you want to settle here and take over. It is your land, Henrietta, but I don't know where we can go. The fruit that was to be saleable has not been enough to keep us."

Henry and Henrietta looked at each other, and she said, "Let us look around outside. It has been so many years since I was here. How many rooms are there?" The response was six rooms and a storage shed out back.

They went outside and walked around the grounds. Neglect was obvious. They looked at each other and decided to offer help. They would stay for a while and then decide. Sam and Sara were both pleased to hear that.

Henrietta said, "We will go back to Oakland and pick up our things. We will be back in three days."

They told Mina about their plan. "We will decide if we can make it work and assist Sara as much as possible."

Henry said he would do what he could. "I have never been a farmer. I was just a kid who followed his father through his workday with the sheep. My mother was the gardener around the house, with a vegetable and flower garden across the front."

Mina told them, "With two of you working there, you will succeed in your efforts." She added that she could lend them a small amount to help if needed. They accepted her offer after a brief trip to retrieve their belongings in San Francisco.

They told Sam to rehire the two previous helpers to assist with tree trimming, removing weak growth in the orchard, and any additional help Henry would need to restore the orchard.

They asked neighboring growers for advice on cultivating fruit growth in the trees. Henrietta spent days tending to Sara and making the house clean and livable. Sara continued to thank Henrietta for her daily help.

Fall came, and the leaves fell. They asked neighbors about feeding the trees in hopes of a good crop in the coming year.

They found their neighbors friendly and told them the growers would all get together over the coming holidays. Henry and Henrietta said they looked forward to it, and they asked how they could do their part.

One morning in October, Henrietta awoke not feeling well.

She asked one of the neighbors for a doctor's recommendation. She had Henry drive her into Woodland.

The doctor checked her and told her she was pregnant. She was in good health, and he provided her with an approximate delivery date.

They drove home with great joy at the news they had to share. Henrietta wrote letters to all.

18

In the fall they had a chance to leave the area as Sara was in stable condition. They told them they were driving to the coast. Henry had checked a map and was interested in coastal land. Henrietta felt well on their trip.

They found lodging for a week in Mendocino. Meals were served twice a day. Each day, they started in a different direction. Talking to people at mealtime was helpful, as many had been in the area for many years.

The community of Mendocino was beautiful to Henrietta, with tiny homes and scenic ocean views, surrounded by Redwood trees to the south.

They found open land. The further south they drove, the more land they saw north of Fort Bragg.

They stopped the car as they saw a large, older house on a hill and a view of the ocean.

Henry was anxious to see a realtor, as there appeared to be no one living in the house. A gate protected it from the road. They drove into Fort Bragg and found a realtor.

Henry asked about the property situated ten miles north. He was told it had been on the market for some time.

The 100-acre property included the hills behind the house. He told them that the owners now lived in Oregon and were eager to sell it.

He escorted Henry and Henrietta around the property.

Henrietta said it looks like a lot of work. The house was

large and looked well-kept, but very dusty from years of no one living there.

Henry told him he had been raised on the north coast of England, and living on the coast again was his wish.

The realtor said he would contact the owner to see if the property was still on the market.

They drove back to Mendocino. Henry was quiet. Henrietta said she would consider getting a loan for the farm to see if that would help with the purchase if Henry was serious about the property.

They arrived just in time for dinner. After they had finished, Henry said he didn't want to put them into debt for his dream.

They went into an art gallery on the way back to their lodging. Art displaying the coastal scenes covered the walls.

A poster on a wall displayed a poem by Carl Koch talking about Mendocino. Henrietta stopped to read it.

> "When the Mendocino sunset
> Turns the western sky to gold
> The ocean's shades and shadows
> Form a shimmering scene untold.
> It's the land of big Paul Bunyan,
> Like the stories told so well
> Farmed redwoods – noble structure
> Always hold you in their spell."

Henrietta and Henry reread it together. He was impressed and told her he enjoyed the area as much as she did.

They returned to Woodland and decided to do their best to make it a profitable venture.

Henry said, "We can't think about the hefty price of land; as we have seen, we can't afford it after our first year as fruit growers."

Henrietta grabbed his hand as they walked and told him she agreed. "After all, we now have an addition to our family to plan for."

He smiled and kissed her cheek.

Henry wrote to his parents about visiting Henrietta's orchard in Woodland and described the conditions they found there.

He told them they had a small loan from Mina, Henrietta's old friend and caregiver from her youth. He explained that it was to rehire the two farm workers. The cousin living there used a wheelchair.

They went to the coast for a few days after settling their affairs. They stayed in a small coastal community called Mendocino.

They traveled south for a few miles and found a 100-acre property with a large home overlooking the sea. They found a realtor who told them it had been vacant for two years.

The realtor said he would contact the owners to see if it was still for sale. The owner lives outside the area, and the realtor did not know why it was vacant.

He explained that they were, he supposed, dreaming, but that piece of property reminded him of home. Henrietta saw the doctor; we expect our first child in about five months.

He ended the letter by saying they hoped they were well.

The months passed quickly. With advice from neighboring growers, Henry was improving the orchard. The returning workers were trimming, fertilizing, and watering; it looked good.

Henrietta planted flowers in the front of the house and a small vegetable garden.

The property owner of the 100-acre ranch by the sea had

contacted them with a price. They told him they were still interested but were restoring their fruit orchard in Woodland and would probably be overextending themselves to purchase the property at this time.

Conversations with the owner lasted several months. They were the only ones interested. Henrietta was feeling well, and the new friends and neighbors, who were farmers' wives, brought her gifts for her baby and visited often.

Just before Christmas, their baby boy was born. They named him Henry, a healthy child. Friends offered a local midwife, and Henrietta coached her through the process.

Henry wrote to his parents and called Mina with the news. They enjoyed their baby. The harvest had been better than it had been in a few years. Henrietta's gardens did well.

Sara continued to lose strength and any desire to eat. She passed away a month after Christmas. Sam continued to help Henry with outside work.

Four months later, Henrietta visited her doctor. She was told she was pregnant again. Henrietta gave birth to her second son on the Woodland farm. They named him William.

Henry had learned a great deal from his neighbors. They saw profits each year and made a large down payment to the owner of the ranch north of Fort Bragg.

The boys were eight and ten when Henry received a letter from his parents that included an estimated cost for a trip home. They were anxious to see the family after all these years. The boys were so excited to take a long train ride followed by a boat excursion.

They planned the trip for the fall after the harvest. Sam was still with them, and he would take care of the property while they were away.

19

Henry and Henrietta were surprised to see how much his parents had aged since their departure after their marriage. They were thrilled to see them and get to know their grandsons. They spent long hours discussing the purchase of their ranch on an installment plan with the owner.

They still hadn't felt comfortable moving on to the property. They had a couple living on the property to watch over the 100 acres, rent-free and with no salary.

"We will move there one day," Henry said. "We go there for long weekends in the summer. The boys love the ocean, climbing the hills behind the house, and fishing with me."

The boys toured the farm with their grandpa, who told them how he tended the sheep.

Henrietta spent time with Henry's mother. She confided in Henrietta about the loneliness they had felt since they left. They worried about the expenses they had in California and wanted to help.

Henry's dad had not told him about their wish to ease their indebtedness.

He was saving that conversation until they had a feeling from Henry's description of the conditions in California and whether their residence would be permanent on the coast, and until they knew which property would allow them to earn a better living for their family. He knew from the distance between the two properties that the decision demanded a choice.

The dinner table conversations with their family were joyful. Henrietta described the boy's activities and interests, noting that the ranch was approximately ten miles from Fort Bragg, where school transportation was provided.

They asked the boys what their favorite animals were. They told them they had a dog. Some of their friends who live on ranches have horses. They hope to have them someday as well.

It became apparent to the grandparents that Henry had not discussed raising sheep with them as he had in his youth. Grandpa took the boys and Henry to his favorite fishing spot. Henry told them he used to fish too.

Henrietta went marketing with Henry's mother to buy food for the days they would be staying there. They baked, shared recipes, and discussed what Grandma cooked when Henry was home and growing up as an active young man.

Henrietta asked if they could visit Lincolnshire and show the boys the area's history. She told Henrietta that it was possible, but Henry's father wished to discuss how they would live when they moved to the ranch and whether they would raise sheep as he had done.

The days went by quickly, and it was a happy time for everyone. Neighbors came by to greet the visiting family. On the last day, Henry and Henrietta were in England, and Henry's father asked them to sit down with him and Henrietta to share thoughts and exchange information.

"We are happy to hear of your progress in the U.S. We wish to know if the farm Henrietta inherited is mortgaged or debt-free."

"It is," they said, "debt-free." They were pleased to hear that.

They then inquired about the amount still owed on the ranch and what they expected to raise or farm on it to make it profitable. Henry stated that they still owed half on the ranch.

His father asked seriously, "What do you plan to do there?"

Henry said, "I plan to raise sheep as you have. I want to raise the long whites. I need to learn more about that from you."

His father said, "You need to have another source of income. With the large property, you can raise cows, horses, or another breed of sheep different from the ones we have raised. I can tell you that Henrietta and I are hard-working and share your goals. Your mother and I have discussed this, and we wish to loan you the money to pay for your indebtedness. Use your money from the farm to stock your ranch and to live on."

Henry and Henrietta were speechless, looking at each other with tears. They told them they appreciated their generosity, assuring them that they would repay them when they could, if that was all right.

They were told that it was agreeable. They went to the bank and were given a check for the agreed-upon amount. The family left, but the boys were not happy to go.

The return on the ship was enjoyable.

The boys met a family going to the U.S. for the first time, who had so many questions. Their family was moving to New York. Henry and William told them they lived on the other side of the country and could not tell them anything about New York, but their mother could, as she had been a nurse there before traveling to England and meeting their father.

The boys told their parents about the family they met and that they would like to speak to their mom about New York.

They boarded the train for their long trip across the country. The boys were restless after a few days. They would walk the length of the train until they reached the boxcars.

Henry read a sign saying, "No admittance."

They turned around to return to their seats when a man emerged from the boxcar. He questioned the boys in a friendly manner, told them he had two horses on the train that he fed daily, and asked if they would like to see them. He took the boys into the boxcar. He told them they were Arabian horses.

The boys had never seen an Arabian horse. Mr. Brown gave the boys a very descriptive talk about the horses. They have distinctly shaped heads, high tail carriages, golden-brown colors, cooperate reasonably well with humans, and are quick to learn. They are the oldest modern breed.

"I have been buying horses for our horse ranch for resale. When I saw these two horses, I bought them as a gift for my wife. She works with me." William asked him to tell their parents about his horses.

He joined the family for dinner that night, where they had a lively discussion about raising horses.

20

Upon returning home, the Smiths learned how the California Gold Rush sparked a surge in migration to the Mendocino Coast.

Soon, others came for the magnificent Redwood Forest, which would provide lumber to rebuild San Francisco after the 1906 Earthquake and fire. Damage had occurred from Monterey to Fort Bragg.

The Union Lumber Company, founded in Fort Bragg, expanded to include milling operations. With the Redwood lumber being exhausted, the lumber company approached the Smiths for permission to cut trees on their 10-Mile Ranch.

The Smith family was reluctant, but their financial circumstances required a change, so they relented and permitted the cutting of Redwoods on their 100 acres.

A few weeks after moving to the ranch, the family had a visitor, Mr. Brown. He came with a horse trailer attached to his pick-up truck.

The boys had come home from school and ran to ask what the horse trailer was doing there.

Mr. Brown and Henry exited their small barn and invited them in.

He had told Henry that his wife was not pleased with his purchase. She said they were in the horse business but not in the novelty-animal business.

The boys were told he was giving them the horses. They

must care for them. He would visit occasionally and check on the horses.

Henry felt he needed more information on the unique breeds of sheep his dad had raised while he was growing up in Lincolnshire, England. He wrote his father a letter asking for help.

His father sent him a great deal of information. As he read and discussed the information with Henrietta, they both felt they had much studying to do before investing in these sheep.

Hebridean Sheep

These unique breeds, the Suffolk Sheep and the Hebridean Sheep, are both native British breeds with distinctive black faces and legs. Although they have similarities, they occupy completely different niches in agriculture.

Hebridean sheep are small, hardy, black-fleeced, and horned. They are low-maintenance, capable of browsing shrubs and thriving on poor, rugged grazing.

Suffolk sheep are large, fast-growing, white-fleeced, meat producers, also known for their superior mutton.

They both needed vegetation to nourish and keep them healthy.

Henrietta suggested, "We should start with the common breed, make some money from them, and grow the vegetation they need to succeed."

Suffolk Sheep

After studying the material on both breeds, they agreed to raise the more marketable Suffolks sheep, not for wool but to sell the meat to butchers and the armed forces.

While Henry wanted to raise these unique sheep as his father had, he realized, after Henrietta told him, that it would take years to produce the ground cover needed to support the Hebridean sheep and produce the desired breeds. It would take more than just fencing them in.

While their property was on the coast like his father's grazing land, they were unprepared for the unique soil and climate of Fort Bragg.

They underestimated the time required to fence the land, plant the right grazing seeds, and acquire the right livestock to start their project.

It was apparent that they had taken on a significant challenge. *(See Appendix C for additional information on the sheep.)*

21

With the distance between the farm in Woodland and the ranch near Fort Bragg, flying would make it possible to manage and supervise the activities on both properties in one day. Finding help in both places proved difficult.

Henry Sr. went to an airfield and asked if they had any small planes that needed repairs to fly. The field manager said he did. Henry explained that he had flown for the R.A.F., was shot down, and discharged; now, he needed the plane to fly from one farm to his ranch to keep everything operational. He had supplied food for the war effort.

The manager looked at Henry and said, "I will give you the plane that requires less work and any parts you may need, and I will transport it at no charge to you."

Henry went home and told Henrietta about the plane he was being given, which needed some work to fly and would be delivered.

Henrietta told him she was pleased with his gift. "I will help with trips to Woodland and report any urgent needs until you have a flying machine again."

Henry cleared a space to repair the plane when it was delivered. While he was an experienced flyer, he was not responsible for keeping the aircraft in good repair.

He went as far as he could, and then he contacted the airfield that had provided him with the plane to obtain the name of the man in charge of plane repairs.

The repair manager told him he would be glad to offer him advice when needed.

It took several months for his plane to be in flying shape. The final task was to cover the aircraft's wings and body. A red oilcloth material was chosen. Two seats were given to him from a wrecked R.A.F. plane brought to the ranch by his long-distance advisor, as he was curious to see the results.

They took off on a trial run. All went well. Henry told his friend that his wife was waiting for the first ride to their farm in Woodland.

Flying again brought back memories of his time as a pilot in the R.A.F. Henry and Henrietta went to see Mina.

They offered her a ride on the plane to see the Bay Area from the air. She thanked them but said her days of adventure were over. "I have to keep my feet on the ground."

The years passed with successful financial returns on the Woodland farm and the Fort Bragg ranch. Henry and Henrietta repaid their parents' generous loan in the early years of their marriage. Their two sons worked on both the ranch and the farm, alongside Henry and Henrietta.

Henry Jr. was eager to learn to fly like his father. William did not want to fly. Henry studied the books available about raising the breed of sheep his grandfather had done, but with little success.

Henry and Henrietta made short trips outside their area to see the northern part of the U.S., leaving the boys in charge.

They continued to give special care to their Arabian horses, gifts from Mr. Brown years ago.

22

———

America entered World War II. The boys wanted to join the country's service. Henry Jr. joined the Army. William was eager to serve his country, but he realized his family needed him to support and help with the two properties. He spoke to friends who were too young to serve. He told them he would help train them in farming or ranch work to help his dad.

William then quietly left to join the Marines, leaving a letter explaining that workers would take his place. Henrietta and Henry were very disappointed that he left in such a way.

Running two properties was challenging for Henry and Henrietta. They missed their sons and watched for their mail.

They raised their sheep to meet military requests. Finding help was a complex process. Losing the pickers when the fruit was ripe was a chore. They advertised for high school students to work on weekends, after school, and during the summer.

Henry made his daily flights from the ranch to the farm. Henrietta oversaw the packing and shipping. Her cousin Sam was still doing his best there.

The news each parent hopes not to receive came to Henrietta and Henry. Their son, William, was killed in the Pacific Theatre of World War II. They were sent a Gold Star and a letter from his commanding officer about his bravery.

Henry received a letter from his mother telling him his dad had passed away and asking him to come home and help her with some decisions she had to make.

Henrietta insisted he make the trip and return as soon as possible. "Ask your mother to come and live with us."

Henrietta found it hard to handle the two properties. She went to Woodland farm to inform Sam and suggested that he ask neighboring farms to offer some workers to help him. He could also advertise for temporary help in the local paper, offering to pay a fair wage.

In England, Henry discovered that his mother was considering selling their land and relocating to town. She would give a portion of the money to Henry and Henrietta, and call their indebtedness paid.

Henry went with his mother to meet her chosen realtor, a long-time friend. She had two helpers to care for the sheep and would stay until the property was sold.

When Henrietta returned home from her trip to Woodland Farm, she opened a letter requesting her help as a nurse at the local hospital in Fort Bragg. A shortage of nurses due to the war required reaching out to retired local nurses.

She replied to the letter, saying she would be happy to come, but her husband was in England because of his father's death. She was managing their ranch, located ten miles north of Fort Bragg, and their farm in Woodland. She would notify them of her starting time after her husband's return.

It was nearly a month before Henry, Sr. returned. He had helped his mother settle in town and witnessed the sale of her farm.

Additionally, the livestock was sold as the new owner informed her that he had other plans.

When he arrived home, he showed Henrietta the check his mother had given him and told her that their indebtedness had been forgiven.

After bringing Henry up to date on her progress tending to

the ranch and farm, she told him about the need for nurses at the local hospital. Henry said that she should do it if she wished.

The hospital administration gave her the night shift. The drive to Fort Bragg was nerve-wracking, as she had to drive without lights on because the road ran along the Pacific coast, and the fear of a Japanese invasion was widespread in the area.

Their schedule was tiring as Henry continued his flight to both the farm and the ranch.

Finding fuel for his plane and Henrietta's drive to Fort Bragg was difficult due to wartime rationing.

23

With the end of the war in 1945 and the return of the service members, life started to return to normal.

Henry Jr. returned and said he wanted to be of help and work on the farm. He also wanted to learn to fly their family plane. His father told him he would teach him on weekends to avoid interfering with his work during the week. Henry Jr. agreed.

Henry Jr. attended a "Welcome Home Dance" in Woodland and met a girl he became interested in. After a month of courting, he brought her home to introduce her to his parents.

Their meeting was cordial. She was raised in Sacramento and had no experience with farm or country life. Shortly after the meeting, they became engaged.

Henrietta told him to bring her to the farm and ranch, show her what her life would be like, and give her a chance to see what her life as a farmer's wife would be like each day.

She came on a Saturday, followed Henry Jr. around as he worked, and spent time at home with Henrietta on meal preparation for the family and hired help.

She stayed in the family house where Sam still lived and continued with the same work as the day before. Each day, she followed Henry Jr. and helped.

This was a new experience as she had been a city girl and her mother had done all the work at home. She expected that Henrietta would do the same.

The wedding was planned, and her family arrived to meet

Henry and Henrietta. Her father ran a hardware store in Sacramento, while her mother managed the home.

Henry and Henrietta offered them the house at Woodland. They would make other arrangements for Sam.

The young couple would be obligated to pay only for utilities, excluding water, since the orchards required a significant amount of water. The arrangement was that Henry and Henrietta still owned the property. They could decorate as they wished.

The bride wanted the wedding in Sacramento, where her family and friends were.

After the wedding, Henry and Henrietta were at the ranch and no longer needed the daily flights.

On an outing, they saw a "For Sale" sign for 400 acres on the property next to theirs. Henry felt he should buy it.

Henrietta questioned their need for more property. He explained that he planned to get more sheep, horses, and chickens and to fence each section.

Henry used the books his father had given him and read about the proper wild growth that the unique sheep would need.

A few months after the war ended, they found it more challenging to sell their marketable sheep, and hoped these specialty sheep would be more profitable. New Zealand and Australia entered the world market by selling lamb.

After selling her property, Henry's mother sent him another check. Henrietta felt she could not question his use of the money. He purchased the 400 acres of land for sale that adjoined their property.

The times were changing for them. Henry Jr. was caring for the farm in Woodland and showing a profit. Henrietta felt he had earned it and should be given the farm, along with the responsibility for paying the yearly taxes on this gift. Henry agreed.

Henry and Henrietta recognized the need to boost their finances by adjusting.

They contacted the lumber company that had purchased their redwood timber and asked whether it was interested in the remaining trees on the property. The lumber company took what they thought was marketable timber and left only stumps behind.

This made raising sheep unreasonable. The lumber company had also been asked to remove the cottages they had built on their land, but never did.

Henry and Henrietta only had Henrietta's salary at this time. They had the two gift Arabian horses, which looked older, but were now seen as pets rather than riding horses.

The stress of feeling "land poor" and getting a bank loan for the first time troubled them. Henrietta always assured Henry that things would get better. She no longer minded her job at the hospital, now that she could work the day shift.

Henry spent his days attempting to remove the stumps but found it hard work. He made trips to the farm to see his grand-children and to help Henry Jr. maintain the orchard. He was given fruit to bring home. He saw little of his daughter-in-law.

Henry was not an experienced cook, but tried to prepare dinner when Henrietta arrived home from nursing.

The manual work took a toll on Henry. The wounds he had received during the war were making his shoulders and back ache with pain at the end of the day.

Henrietta told him to quit the hard work and rest to regain his strength, and she would care for him. He said he would, but he felt it was wrong that Henrietta was the "breadwinner" and responsible for them.

24

Henry Jr. came to the house one day in his truck with fruit and produce from his garden. He found his dad on the ground with his ax in his hand. He was conscious and told Henry Jr. he could not get up.

Henry carried his father into the house and looked for the doctor's number. He called Henrietta at the hospital.

The doctor was there when she arrived home. He told her it was Henry's heart and that he could no longer do the work he had been doing.

She told the doctor about their talk, but obviously, he had not done what she asked.

Henrietta asked her son why he had made the trip during the week.

He told her that on his father's previous trip to the farm, he thought that his father did not look well. He had experienced a brief period of weakness and then rested before flying back home.

Henrietta told him she would take care of him. She gave notice to the hospital that she could no longer work there because of her husband's illness. She spent as much time with Henry as she could.

When cooking a meal, she made enough for two to three days' worth. She planted a vegetable garden for their use and asked her son to fence off a small part of the property behind the house for chickens and a small coop for laying eggs.

She also requested that Henry Jr. build a porch on the front of the house so his dad could be outside and enjoy the sun on warm days.

Henry Jr. did as his mother asked him. Having him on the property with them and talking with his dad comforted her.

Henry Jr. was taking flying lessons as often as he could. The drive to the ranch was time-consuming, and the farm work was seasonal. His wife resented the time he spent on the ranch.

Henrietta liked the time she had with Henry. It took her back to those first days in the hospital in London. She knew Henry would not recover and would no longer travel off the ranch.

Henry was the love of her life. She was as cheerful as she could be with him, encouraging him to be in good spirits.

They liked to sit together on the porch on warm evenings, listen to the crickets and frogs near their pond, and look at the stars. They talked about William and what he might have done if he were still with them.

Henrietta wrote a letter to Henry's mother asking her to come for a visit if she was up to it, telling her it would lift his spirits and her own to see him.

Henry's mother wrote back to Henrietta, telling her she was not well enough for such a trip but would write to Henry more often.

Henrietta wrote to Mina, whom she had not heard from in a while. She received a reply letter from Mina, which she could not write herself; a neighbor had written it.

Henrietta was torn between wanting to be there for Mina and for Henry's care.

Henrietta had visits from friends in Woodland whom Henry had made on his first arrival there. Henrietta was so pleased with their visits.

Henry Jr.'s wife had another child, but did not invite Henrietta to visit. She did not understand her daughter-in-law's coolness to her. Henry Jr. brought his son to see his grandma and grandpa and brought a small cake for them.

Their visits on the front porch to watch the sunsets over the ocean were becoming difficult for Henry.

Henrietta was not strong enough to support Henry's weight as he leaned on her to move about in the house. She gave him a sponge bath daily and a bath in their tub on Saturdays when Henry Jr. was available.

Henry Jr. received his flying license, and flying to the ranch became easier as the state had built a wider roadway along the coast in recent years. The old highway was left in sections as a daytime-only landing strip.

The sound of the plane landing brought smiles to Henry and Henrietta.

25

———

Henry soon passed peacefully. Sometime after his passing, I learned that Henrietta had attempted to follow her husband's work of digging up the stumps left in the ground by the lumber company's neglect.

Instead of digging, she tried to burn them out. She stepped into a hole that was still burning and suffered a burn that required hospitalization.

She decided it would be in her best interest to move back to Oakland.

Yet, she had a few weeks of recovery at home before she could make the move. Unfortunately, she didn't arrive in Oakland in time to be with Mina before she passed.

Henrietta was in touch with her old nursing friends when she came back to Oakland. She had been invited to a cocktail party by a friend. It was an afternoon affair. She was loudly welcomed by her friends: "Happy is here!"

Henrietta was introduced to a visiting writer, James. His mother had been a nurse at Fabiola. Henrietta was of the class of 1917. He sat beside Henrietta and said he would like to meet with "The Fabiola Girls." Henrietta said she would call him.

She told James the Fabiola Girls would be meeting in six months. They are the alumni group from the opening of the first hospital, built in 1876.

In 1974, on the day of the Fabiola Girls Reunion, James picked her up, and they went to the gathering. The home for the Fabiola Girls reunion was beautiful and set on a mountain.

The hostess was Ruth Leidsen Swanson, a member of the class of 1928.

When the door opened, he kissed Henrietta on the cheek and said, "This is my date." Henrietta introduced him as James P. O'Neil, a writer for the Montclarion newspaper, whose mother had attended nursing school years ago.

They were ushered into the living room, and Henrietta introduced James to the group's secretary, Gladys. The crowd seemed to range in age from seventy to ninety. He saw seventy women, all dressed to the hilt.

Henrietta and Gladys reminisced that 50 years ago, they were in training. "We received $5.00 a month and were charged $.10 cents for library fees."

Henrietta's lovely face creased into a grin as she said, "They also took out $1.00 if we broke a thermometer. From our monthly $5.00 'salary', aprons and uniforms had to be purchased."

Henrietta sat James down next to an older lady. She told him that she was ninety-two.

He said, "You don't look it." She tapped his knee and said, "Don't fool me, son." They brought out picture albums from their days at Fabiola.

26

We talked to Henrietta each time we were outside, asking her to come and have dinner with the family.

She was always cheerful and shared wonderful stories to the children's pleasure. She took a genuine interest in their lives.

One day, she brought me some quince from her tree. I had never seen a quince, so I asked her what I should do with them. She gave me a jam recipe.

She sat down for a cup of tea and a slice of my Gravenstein apple pie. I had bought the apples from a roadside stand on our way home from Joe's sister's place at the Russian River.

Henrietta asked me if I had always wanted to be a stay-at-home mom. I told her no. I had imagined myself as a nurse.

I was not encouraged or supported in my wish to do that when I graduated from high school in 1946. My father would not sign the paperwork or help me.

I was dating Joe, and he didn't think I should work outside the home. Henrietta told me I could do it now. I told her, "I think it is too late with four children."

A few days later, Henrietta came over with Henry Jr. She said she would fly to the ranch with Henry and stay a few weeks. He said, "I will bring her back."

It was two months before they returned, bringing a case of apricots and plums.

She asked me if I was feeling well. I told her I was not, that I was pregnant.

A few days later, she came to our house and gave me a baby gift and an enclosed card with a poem she had written:

> *Dear June,*
> *I've noticed lately, neighbor dear,*
> *By your expanding girth,*
> *Your increasing, multiplying, and*
> *Replenishing the earth.*
> *I bring this gift, in token*
> *Of my sincerest joy,*
> *That you'll soon present the neighbor*
> *With another baby boy.*
> *Henrietta Smith*

Front of the Card to June from Henrietta

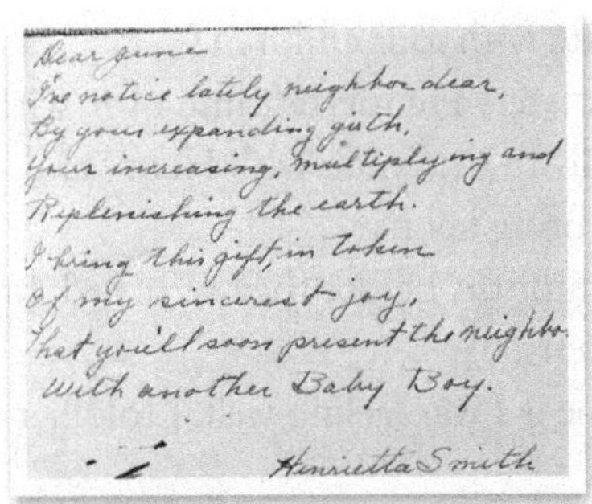

Henrietta's poem for June

Henrietta asked me to attend a luncheon of the "Fabiola Girls" so I could ask questions about their nursing. As we entered the restaurant's dining room, a woman yelled, "Happy is here!"

Henrietta introduced me as a potential nurse. They talked to me, telling me they were never sorry they had gone into nursing. Having spoken to current nurses, they find it less challenging due to the efforts of nurses' organizations, which have secured better salaries and working conditions.

It was a lovely afternoon. I thanked Henrietta and told her that when I could, I would look into it again and see if, at my age, I could apply.

Back to Front: Jeff, Scott, Joe, Me (June), Chris, Lynn, and Gail

The children were growing up and discussing college plans for after they finished high school. I knew we could not support five children in college on one salary.

As the years passed, our friendship with Henrietta continued to grow. We made sure she was not alone on the holidays. Usually, within four or five days after Thanksgiving or Christmas, Henry Jr. would drive his family from Woodland to

Oakland. They would stand on the sidewalk in front of her house, waiting for her to come out. She would then walk them to the corner, to a Chinese buffet restaurant, and treat them to dinner before returning home.

One time, she invited us to come to the ranch for a weekend. We drove her with us on a Friday after Joe had finished work.

It was a long drive. The kids were excited to go and see the Arabian horses they had heard so much about. As we drove through the countryside to the coastal road ten miles north of Fort Bragg, we passed a farm with clothing on the line.

Henrietta made a statement that has stayed with me.

Looking out the window, she said, "Oh, the banners of poverty." I told her I'd read that in a novel. I think it was by John Steinbeck.

As we arrived at the ranch, it was already dark. Henry Jr. was standing at the side of the road. He directed Joe to keep his car headlights on and aim them north so he could take off on the narrow runway and fly before the expected fog arrived.

We spent the night in the house. Henry Jr.'s son had been there during the day and prepared the house for our visit. It had been empty for some time.

Henrietta was up early. I heard her on the phone with a friend, asking him to bring her two abalones for breakfast because she had guests who would enjoy them. The fisherman brought the abalone, and Henrietta prepared them for our breakfast.

After breakfast, we walked along a path to see some cottages that the lumber company had built for its employees during the years of redwood cutting. There was still an example of a home of a "pack rat." You could not walk in as it was filled with paper and trash.

We examined the stumps throughout the property. Only

one of the Arabian horses was left in the yard, and another was a workhorse.

From the front porch, you could look out over the ocean and the new highway as a few cars passed by.

Henrietta looking at the fields on her ranch

Joe drove Henrietta and me into town while our children looked for shells on the beach. As we entered the grocery store, Henrietta had a weak spell, and as I turned my back, she was on the floor.

I told her we should go home, she could give me her grocery list, and I would come back and do her shopping.

She said that would be helpful. She wanted to spend a few days at the ranch, and Henry Jr. could fly her back to Oakland.

27

Ten days later, she came back to Oakland, a little pale, but on her feet.

She asked me to drive her to San Francisco to see a doctor there whom her doctor had recommended.

We made the trip to San Francisco.

After her doctor's visit, she wanted to visit a friend on Clement Street, a young woman who had grown up in Woodland on a neighboring farm.

She was a flight attendant. She made us French onion soup and fancy ham-and-cheese sandwiches.

It was an enjoyable day for me.

For Henrietta, it was not. Her doctor's visits were depressing for her. She was told to limit her activity. No more plane rides with her son.

Henry Jr. came to see his mother the next day. He wanted to take her to Woodland and find a care facility.

She told him she was not ready to give up. She would stay in Oakland a while longer with her next-door friends.

My mother had been staying with us. She went through a period of not feeling well, with leg pain and discomfort.

Henrietta came over, applied warm packs, and spoke with her.

She helped my mother rearrange her finances so she would have enough to live in her home again.

Before my mother left to return home, we had Henrietta over more frequently.

Josephine (June's mother), **Henrietta***, Jill
(June's daughter-in-law), and Joe (June's
husband)*

One day, she brought a beautiful shawl to my mother. She said it has a history. This was the precious Kashmiri paisley shawl her mother-in-law had given her.

A few days after my mother moved back to her home in La Mesa, Henrietta came over and told me she had decided to return to the ranch while she and Henry Jr. found a place for her in Woodland.

She asked if I would drive her to the Hayward airport. Henry would land there and take her to the ranch.

I told her I would. She got into the car. She had little to say except that she had decided she could no longer live alone. She was not yet ready for a care facility, but Henry Jr. was looking for an apartment in Woodland for her.

As I pulled into the airport, I saw the little red plane sitting on the field, waiting for Henrietta. She exited the car, wearing a trimmed hat and a black coat, carrying her little black suitcase.

Turning, she said, "Come and see me in Woodland." I told

her I would. She climbed into the plane and sat next to Henry. She looked out the window and waved. I knew I would never forget that moment.

Henry rented a room with a bath in a senior residence where meals were served. We drove there on a Sunday after hearing from Henry.

She was only there for three weeks before she was moved to a care facility. Henry called to say she was there.

We told him we would be there the following weekend. He provided us with instructions on how to find it. A nurse directed us to her.

As we walked down the hall near her room, Henrietta called, "Henry, is that you?" When I heard that, I wondered if she was calling the love of her life or Henry Jr, the son who spent so much time with his mother, whom he always wanted to please.

Henrietta's life was not an easy one. As a child, she had concerns: Where will I sleep, and who will care for me? Her mother did her best to supply a roof over their heads and food on the table.

While she did not wish to burden Henrietta with the difficult decisions she had to make, Henrietta knew life was not as she would like it to be because of her father's injuries during the time he was enlisted in the army and his attempted recovery at home.

As a teenager, Henrietta experienced some loneliness with the passing of her mother. Mina was always there for her and did her best to assure Henrietta that she was loved.

Henrietta learned and taught many life lessons by example, helping others to lead happy lives.

She emphasized the importance of taking advantage of each opportunity, recognizing that we must make numerous decisions throughout our lifetime. We can choose to appreciate our surroundings and friends, make friends with those who need a friend, and strive to be as cheerful as possible. Be pleasant and positive rather than negative. Thank your Heavenly Father for all that comes your way.

Three wars affected Henrietta for some time: the loss of her parents, the loss of her son William in WWII, and, in later years, her husband, as his WWI injuries hampered his activities in maintaining the ranch.

She appreciated being included in our family and the affection our children, Joe, and I had for her. She showed her son affection in many ways.

My son, Scott, made home movies that included his sisters, brothers, sister-in-law, and Henrietta. She volunteered and found joy in doing it.

Henrietta helped anyone whom she felt she could. She left joy behind her. I learned a great deal from Henrietta – to be genuinely interested in people and willing to listen.

She had asked her son to bring two cases of apricots and plums to our house. She came over to tell me to expect them. She sat down and had a cup of tea and cookies that my girls and I had made.

She asked me again if I had always wanted to be a stay-at-home wife. I told her no. I shared that I had seen a movie with my mother about the building of the Panama Canal and the health issues at that time. The work of a nurse and a doctor corrected them. I decided then that I wanted to be a nurse.

After graduating from high school, I visited the nearest hospital that offered a nursing program and requested an application. They asked my age. I was 17. They told me I needed my parents' approval at that age.

I took the application home and asked my father for his signature. He refused and tore it up. I was dating Joe at the time, and he said I didn't need to work outside the home if we got married.

I told Henrietta my story.

She told me I could do it now if I were still interested.

I told her I was still curious but afraid I was too old; however, I would look into it.

I did not confide in her and tell her I thought I was pregnant with my 5th child.

I was 34 years old when this conversation took place. I told her about my desire to drive and the challenges of obtaining support and enrolling our children in preschool so they could learn to play with other children.

She told me it all depends on how you feel; it is essential. I had been thinking about our conversation for a long time.

My fifth child, Chris, was three years old when I enrolled him in the same preschool that his brothers and sisters had attended. I had learned to drive seven years before.

I signed up for the local nursing school, worked in hospitals for 27 years, and finally served as the only nurse for 12 years in a doctor's office.

Thank you to Henrietta for her influence on me.

After retiring and moving to Southern California, I volunteered at the local hospital for seventeen years.

I look back on it now as time well spent.

As I drove to the hospital, I often thought of Henrietta and how she was always willing to give her time to those in need, whether family, friends, or acquaintances.

Her cheerful attitude was always present. She left us with a spirit of caring and kindness to others in our lives.

APPENDIX A

THE SAN FRANCISCO
FAIR AND EXHIBITION

The land for the fair was chosen on the edge of the bay, and the entrance was to be on Scott Street. The walls were covered with living grass. Vertical lawns were planted 30 feet high on the street side of Scott Street. The ice plant was planted 30 feet high and 11 feet long.

Visitors to Stirling Calder's "Fountain of Energy" were transported by trolley car or ferry boat. The garden featured ornamental sculptures and continuous blooms of International Grand Prize Roses. There was also the California building, where Luther Burbank displayed his new varieties of fruit and flowers, and where California's diversity was showcased in the Horticultural Palace with a spectacular glass dome.

The many exhibits included the following:

- Japanese Pavilion, Rose Garden, Japanese Temple, and teahouses.
- Canadian Pavilion – a large diorama showing the prairies, crops, wildlife, and transportation that traveled across the country.
- Siam – a reconstructed pavilion from Siam, exotic and so different.
- Guatemala – its marimba music

- Italy – Italian art, flowers, fountains, wicker baskets, and chairs to see the grounds that ran on a battery that could be rented for $1.00.
- Portugal showed its elaborate architecture. "Have a cold drink."
- Washington State received a can of salmon on one day of celebration.
- Cadillac ambulances belonged to the service building hospital and were equipped with the latest medical equipment to treat falls, fainting, and other medical emergencies, and were staffed by volunteers.
- Blackfoot Indians provided entertainment sponsored by the Great Northern Railroad and Glacier National Park.
- Japan gave kite-flying instructions.
- The suffrage booth by Women's Suffrage - Thousands signed the Suffrage Amendment before Congress. It was not until 1920, with the passing of the 19th Amendment, that all American Women had the right to vote.
- Souvenirs available were pillows, spoons, scarves, and jewelry
- "The End of the Trail Sculpture" – a dying Indian on a tired horse showed the failure of the Indians to save their lands – "A moving piece."
- John Philip Sousa played marching music, etc.
- Ice cream was ten cents.
- Auto-trains moved visitors around the grounds – 5-10 cents
- French and Japanese pavilions with models of beautiful silk gowns against a backdrop of gardens at Versailles. Rodin's statue of the "Thinker" was in front.

- John McLaren, who had designed Golden Gate Park, was hired as the Master Landscaper.
- The land for the fair was chosen on the edge of the bay, and the entrance was to be on Scott Street. The walls were covered with living grass. Vertical lawns were planted 30 feet high on the street side of Scott Street. The ice plant was planted 30 feet high and 11 feet long.
- Visitors to Stirling Calder's "Fountain of Energy " were transported by trolley car or ferry boat. The garden featured ornamental sculptures and continuous blooms of International Grand Prize Roses.
- There was also the California building, where Luther Burbank displayed his new varieties of fruit and flowers, showcasing California's diversity in the Horticultural Palace, which featured a spectacular glass dome.
- "The Aladdin of 1915" was designed and lit by W. Dorcy, featuring indirect lighting with searchlights. The spacious and beautiful gardens were surrounded by buildings that showcased their culture, music, and fine arts. Sculptors and painters with worldwide reputations were hired to participate.

APPENDIX B

THE MEXICAN REVOLUTION

The Mexican Revolution continued for several years under new and different leaders, with Diaz in power for the longest period, over 30 years, keeping the peons in poor condition.

In January 1916, at Santa Isabel, Chihuahua, a train from El Paso, Texas, was going to Denver with American engineers and technicians. The train was stopped and boarded, and 15 people were murdered, and others were wounded.

In March, Villa sent 485 men across the border into Columbus, New Mexico. They terrorized people, shot several, and set the town on fire. Some Americans traveled south to the border to seek revenge but were arrested and put into Mexican jails.

This was one of the events that sparked Mother Jones' interest.

APPENDIX C
THE SHEEP

The Hebridean Sheep

The books that Lincolnshire Trust provided were given to Henry, Sr. by his mother after his father's death. The two main breeds raised were the Hebridean and the Suffolks.

In 1993, the Hebridean was used to control birch scrub and invasive tussock grasses, and to promote heather regeneration in Yorkshire. In 1995, The Trust had the world's largest flock of pedigree Hebrideans. By 1999, the flock had stabilized at over 100 breeding ewes, producing 120 to 140 lambs yearly. The flock is maintained at the peak level of around 27 sheep.

The public has shown interest in black, wild-looking sheep with horns, while schoolchildren bottle-feed baby lambs to connect with farm animals and understand the importance of conserving wild habitats.

The Ortum Pedigree Suffolk Sheep

This flock of Pedigree Suffolk was started in 1978 with 10 animals. Soon, Henry and Henrietta purchased Rams, and in a few years, they had 20 females. Within a short time, they had 8-12 head of long-bodied white lambs.

After the war, they had to compete with Australia and New Zealand to sell their lambs in America. The knitters, spinners, and weavers look forward to the beautiful, fine wool for their yarn, which enables them to produce high-quality articles.

ABOUT THE AUTHOR

I started writing this book several years ago as we drove home from Woodland, California, after saying our last goodbye to Henrietta.

It was a busy time in our home. I was nursing at various hospitals. Our children were making college choices, pursuing careers, getting married, and serving missions in Scotland and Peru.

June Ehorn, 2025

I took my book out from time to time and put it away.

After the loss of my son, Jeff, and my husband, Joe, I decided it was time to complete my book and remember our good times. Now, at 97, I have completed this happy project!

ACKNOWLEDGMENTS

I would not have continued this story if not for the encouragement of my daughters, Gail and Lynn.

Their knowledge of writing was very helpful. Gail spent many hours on this project, and often called her sister, Lynn, in Utah, to discuss my work.

I am grateful to my granddaughter, Elisa, for her time and talents in the book design. I will forever be grateful for their interest and help.

June, with her daughters, Gail and Lynn.

BIBLIOGRAPHY

Lincolnshire Wildlife Trust. *Grazing of Hebridean Sheep.* Horncastle, Lincolnshire, England.

Travel Assistance for the Heart of England, including Historic Houses, Gardens, Shakespeare Country, The Cotswolds, and Castles.

Walters, Shipley. *Woodland, a City of Trees.* 1920. History of the development of the area from wilderness to the dawn of a new century.

Oakland City Library. History of Oakland. Development of the future Dimond District Park.

O'Neil, James P. *The Story of the Fabiola Girls.* Montclarian, 1978.

Fabiola Hospital, class of 1915-1917. Henrietta's time in nursing school.

Barker, Malcom. *Three Fearful Days: San Francisco Memoirs of the 1906 Earthquake and Fire.* San Francisco: Londonborn Publications, 1998.

1915 Fair and Exposition. San Francisco Invites the World. Events to be seen on pamphlets and newspapers of 1915.

Orturn flock of pedigree Suffolk sheep. Long bodies, long white hair.

Cranwell College. Near Lincoln, 1917. Taught flying, training for the R.A.F.

Fort Bragg. History of the lumber industry, 1920-1956.

Sheep ranching 1920-1950. Henry is on a trip to Mendocino.

Dimond Park is named for the Gold Rush. Montclarian, May 2, 2000.

Dunn, Eleanor. *A Short History of Dimond Campers and Sausal Creek.*

Indian Tribes

Life on Sausal Creek 1868-1888.

Excerpts from Casper Hawkins, 1948. California Historical Society Quarterly 271, 65573.

Maternity – History of the Practice Recorded by MCA 1918-1958.

Jones, Mary Harris. *Autobiography of Mother Jones.* New York: Dover Publications, Inc., 2004.

Magazine articles on Mother Jones and the Mexican Revolution.

May, Michael C., Witheron Sherman, and Susan M. Deeds. *The Course of Mexican History.*

Randolph Dilefanty. Chronicle Books, 1995. Discusses the clock tower and the San Francisco Ferry Building.

Made in the USA
Monee, IL
07 July 2026

56551551R00075